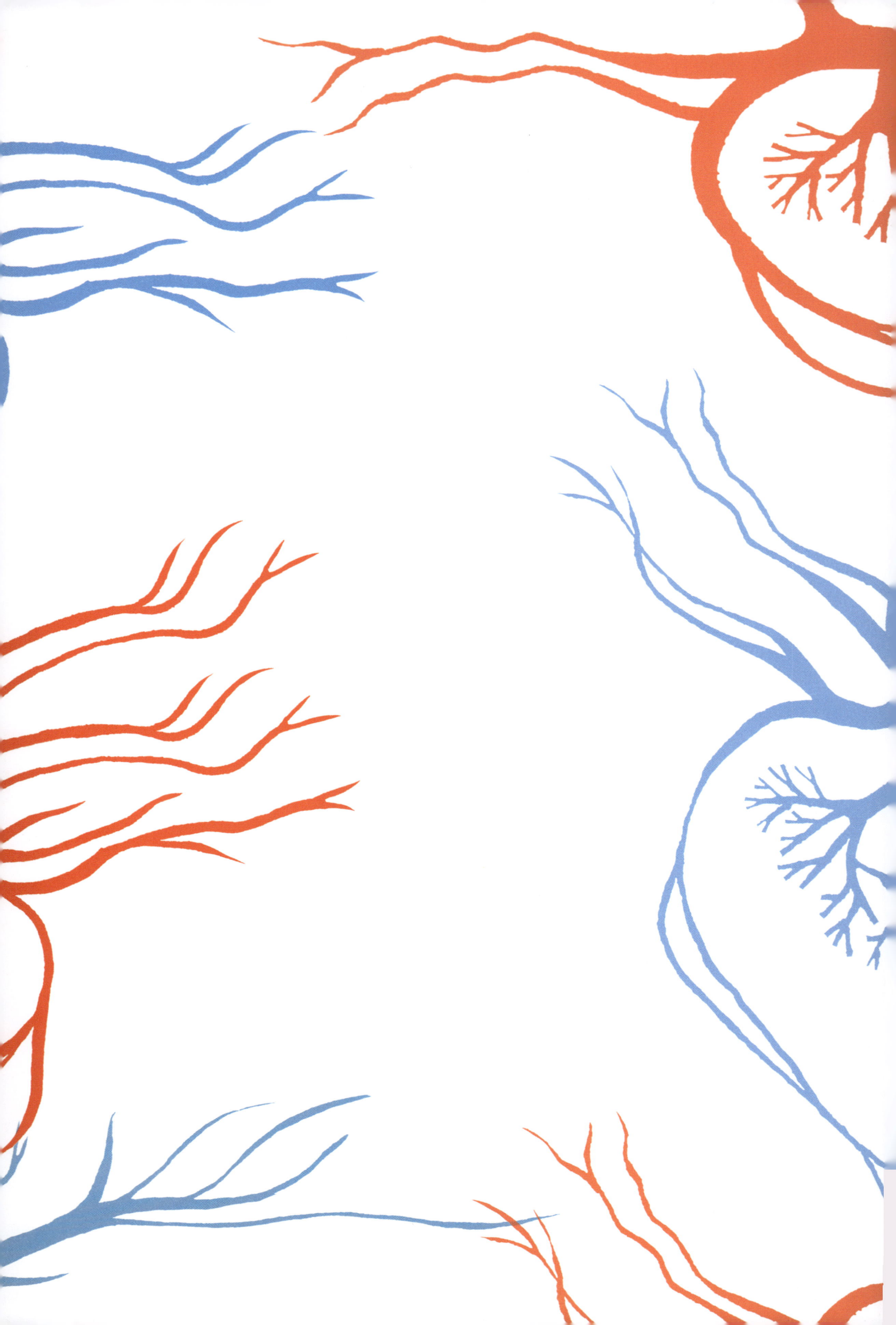

THE MARVELLOUS ADVENTURE OF BEING HUMAN

WRITTEN BY **DR MAX PEMBERTON**
ILLUSTRATED BY **CHRIS MADDEN**

wren & rook

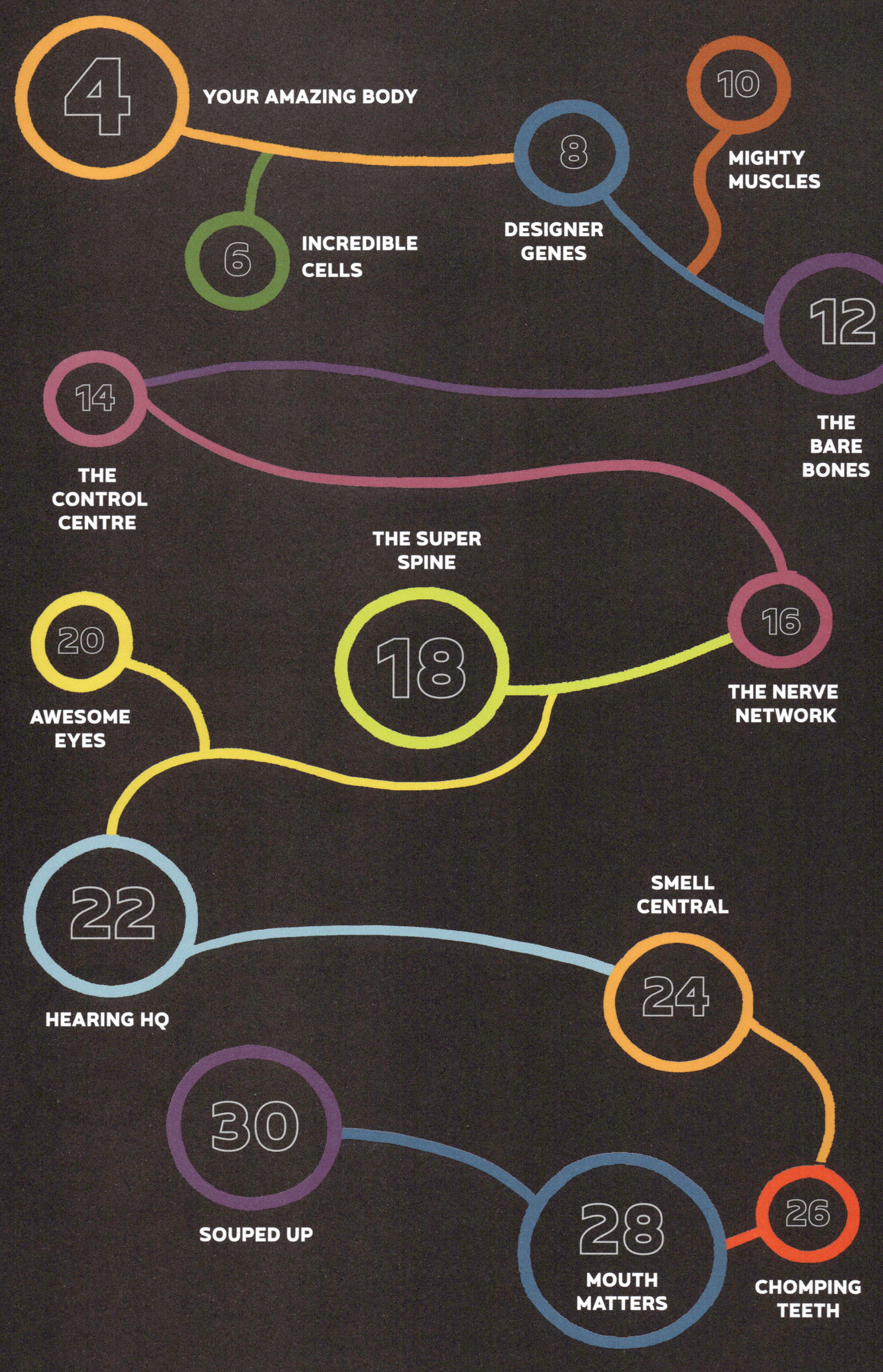

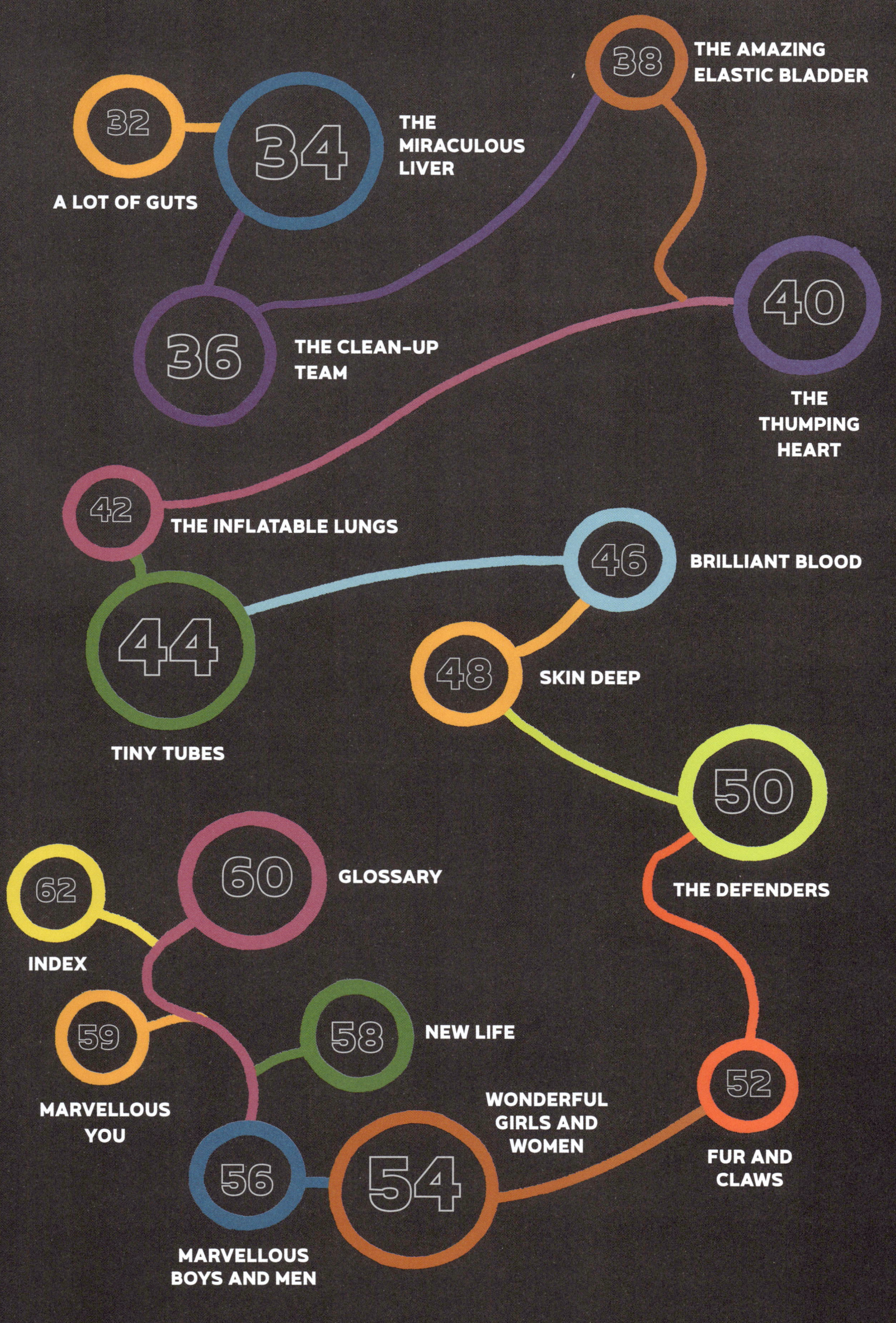

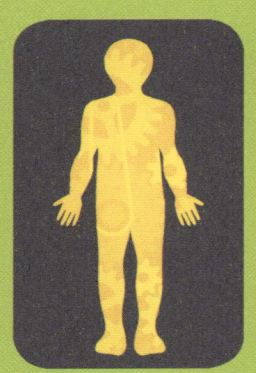

When I trained to become a doctor, I spent a long time learning about the body – but even now, many years later, I'm still astonished by how clever it is. Yet many of us don't know very much about it. We spend our lives trusting that our bodies will keep us moving and breathing, without thinking about the incredible processes going on inside us. The truth is that the cells, tissues and organs in our bodies are hard at work all the time – and without them, we wouldn't be alive.

YOUR AMAZING BODY

Shrink yourself down as small as you can go. No – much smaller than that! You'll need to be small enough to crawl up a nostril, peer inside an eyeball and float through the bloodstream, because you're coming with me on a fascinating journey around the human body. We'll discover how all the different organs and systems fit and work together to make one of the most amazing creatures in the universe – you!

It's easy to take your body for granted, but by the end of your microscopic journey, I hope you'll realise how extraordinary and special it is. You'll find out all about how the body fights back when it's under attack from germs and poisons, how it's developed cunning ways to keep you safe, and how the food that you eat affects how well your organs function. I believe in the saying, 'look after your body and it will look after you', and you'll find my suggestions on how to keep happy and healthy in the Body Boost sections in this book.

So, are you ready to come with me on an adventure, exploring your **AMAZING BODY** and how to live in it? Let's go!

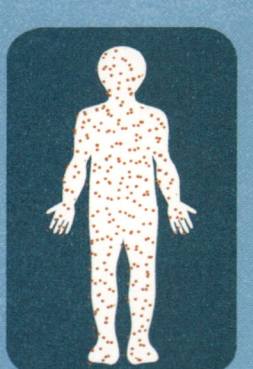

Your amazing human body is made up of bones, blood, tissue and organs that work together to protect you and help you grow. Let's start our adventure by taking a close-up look at what all of those individual parts are made of – cells.

INCREDIBLE CELLS

Now that we're small enough to travel around inside a human body, we can see the cells that make it up – at normal size we'd need a microscope. Cells are the building blocks of a body. Just like a house is built from thousands of bricks, a human body is made up of TRILLIONS of cells. Each cell is made up of different parts that keep it alive, such as the cell membrane, cytoplasm and nucleus.

CELL MEMBRANE
Keeps the cell together, and allows oxygen and nutrients in, and waste products, such as carbon dioxide, out.

CYTOPLASM
Jelly-like substance that fills the cell. Tiny structures in cytoplasm allow material to travel about the cell, digest nutrients, or release energy.

NUCLEUS
The cell's instructions are stored here.

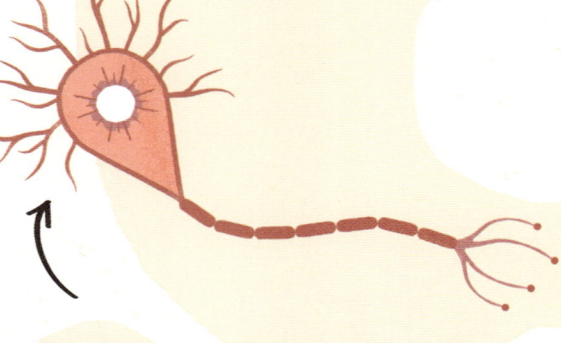

There are about 200 different varieties of cell in your body. This is a nerve cell, which helps us feel sensations such as touch and pain by carrying messages from one part of our body to another.

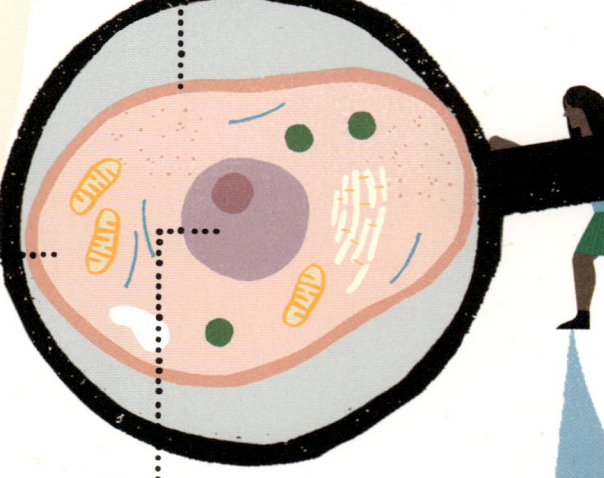

This red blood cell zooms around the body carrying oxygen. It is round and flat making it the ideal shape for absorbing lots of oxygen.

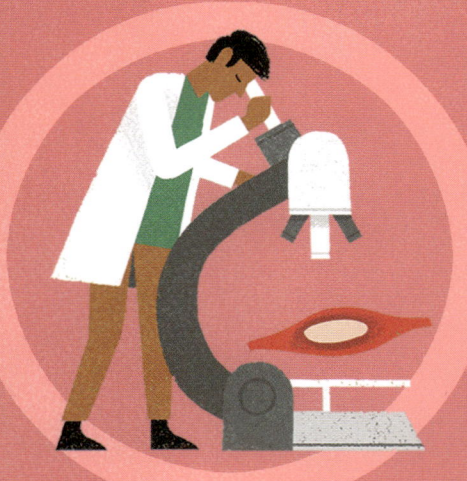

 Each **CELL** is pretty amazing on its own, but when cells join up, incredible things happen.

BODY BOOST

Your cells grow old and die all the time! Don't worry though, your body makes enough new ones to replace them just as quickly. Eating foods with lots of protein, such as fish, nuts and eggs, will keep your new cells healthy.

 Cells doing the same job work together in groups called **TISSUE**.

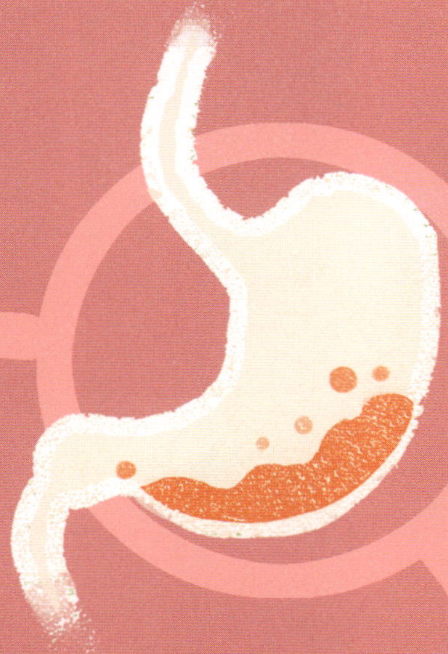

 An **ORGAN**, such as your stomach, is made up of different types of tissue. Some organs have just one job – your eyes help you to see, for instance. But other organs have lots – the liver does more than 500 tasks!

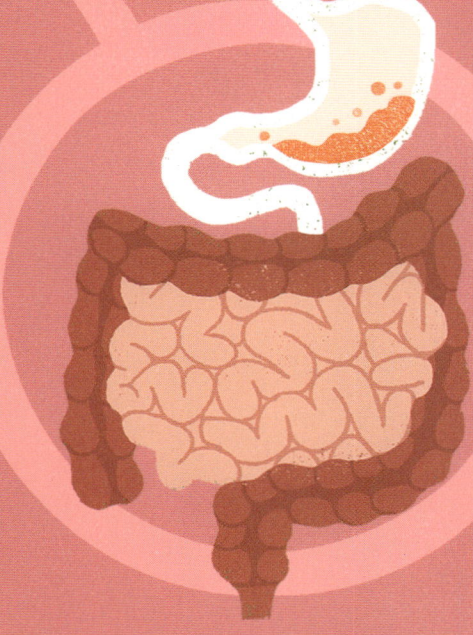

So your body is made up of all sorts of different parts but, whatever they do, they have one thing in common – all of them are made of cells!

 Different organs work together in **SYSTEMS** that help the body to function. For example, the stomach is part of the digestive system, which also includes the oesophagus, or gullet, and intestines.

7

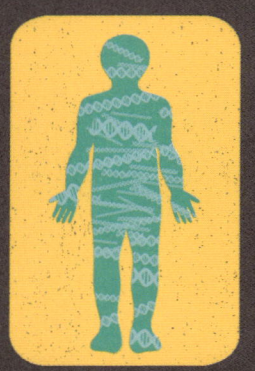

Get ready to shrink down even more for this next bit, because we're about to peer right inside a cell's nucleus, which controls what the cell does. Inside the nucleus is a sort of human being instruction manual in the form of a chemical called deoxyribonucleic acid, or DNA for short. Individual instructions in DNA – telling your hair to be straight or curly, for example – are called genes.

DESIGNER

Your DNA determines everything about you, from the way you look to whether you're a boy or a girl. The instructions in DNA – the genes – are slightly different in everyone, so people are all different. Variations in genes are the reason why some people have blue eyes and others have brown eyes, or why some people are tall and others are short.

If you look closely at the DNA inside the nucleus of the cell, you'll see that it's tightly coiled and twisted. Amazingly, if we were to take hold of each end of the DNA strand in just one cell and pull it out straight, it would measure two metres long!

THERE'S LOTS OF DNA IN EVERY SINGLE CELL IN YOUR BODY!

Your genes come from your parents, so things such as red hair or green eyes run in families, passed from one generation to the next. The way the genes are mixed is unique to you, which is why brothers and sisters with the same parents look different from one another. The only people in the world with exactly the same genes are identical twins!

GENES

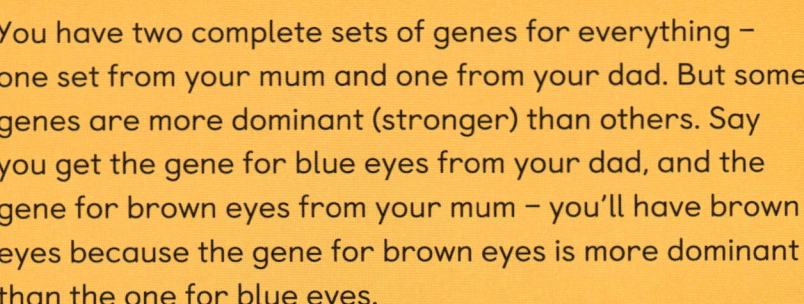

Dad has red hair, but mine is brown like Mum's. Roughly 2 per cent of the population have red hair!

All living things have DNA, from plants to insects. Humans have about 98.8 per cent of the same genes as a chimpanzee!

You have two complete sets of genes for everything – one set from your mum and one from your dad. But some genes are more dominant (stronger) than others. Say you get the gene for blue eyes from your dad, and the gene for brown eyes from your mum – you'll have brown eyes because the gene for brown eyes is more dominant than the one for blue eyes.

But that doesn't mean you can only have brown-eyed children yourself, as you would still have one blue-eye gene and one brown-eye gene. This means you could pass on the blue-eye gene to your child. And if the other parent also passes on a blue-eye gene, then your child would have blue eyes!

Apart from when they ache after a game of football, you might not give your muscles too much thought. But they're working all the time, controlling every single movement your body makes. As well as moving your legs for that sensational tackle, muscles do lots of jobs that you don't think about, from keeping your heart pumping to allowing your lungs to move so that you can breathe.

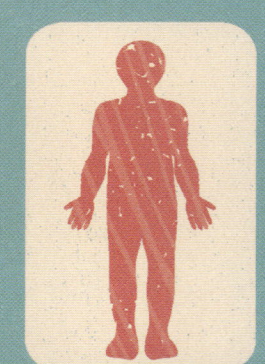

MIGHTY MUSCLES

If you take a close look at a muscle, you'll see that it's made of stretchy tissue that works a bit like elastic. But not all muscles are the same. Let's look at the three different types.

① The muscles that make Superman super-strong are called **SKELETAL MUSCLES**. These are the muscles that provide the power for actions such as walking or smiling. They're attached to your bones by tough cords called tendons, and together they form our musculoskeletal system. These are the only muscles that we deliberately control by thinking about them.

Skeletal muscles often ache if you use them a lot, like on a long bike ride. That's because muscles get tiny rips in them when they've worked extra hard. Although that sounds nasty, our bodies are very good at repairing these miniscule tears. In fact, once the muscle has repaired itself, it will usually be even bigger and stronger – that's why doing exercise gets easier the more you do it.

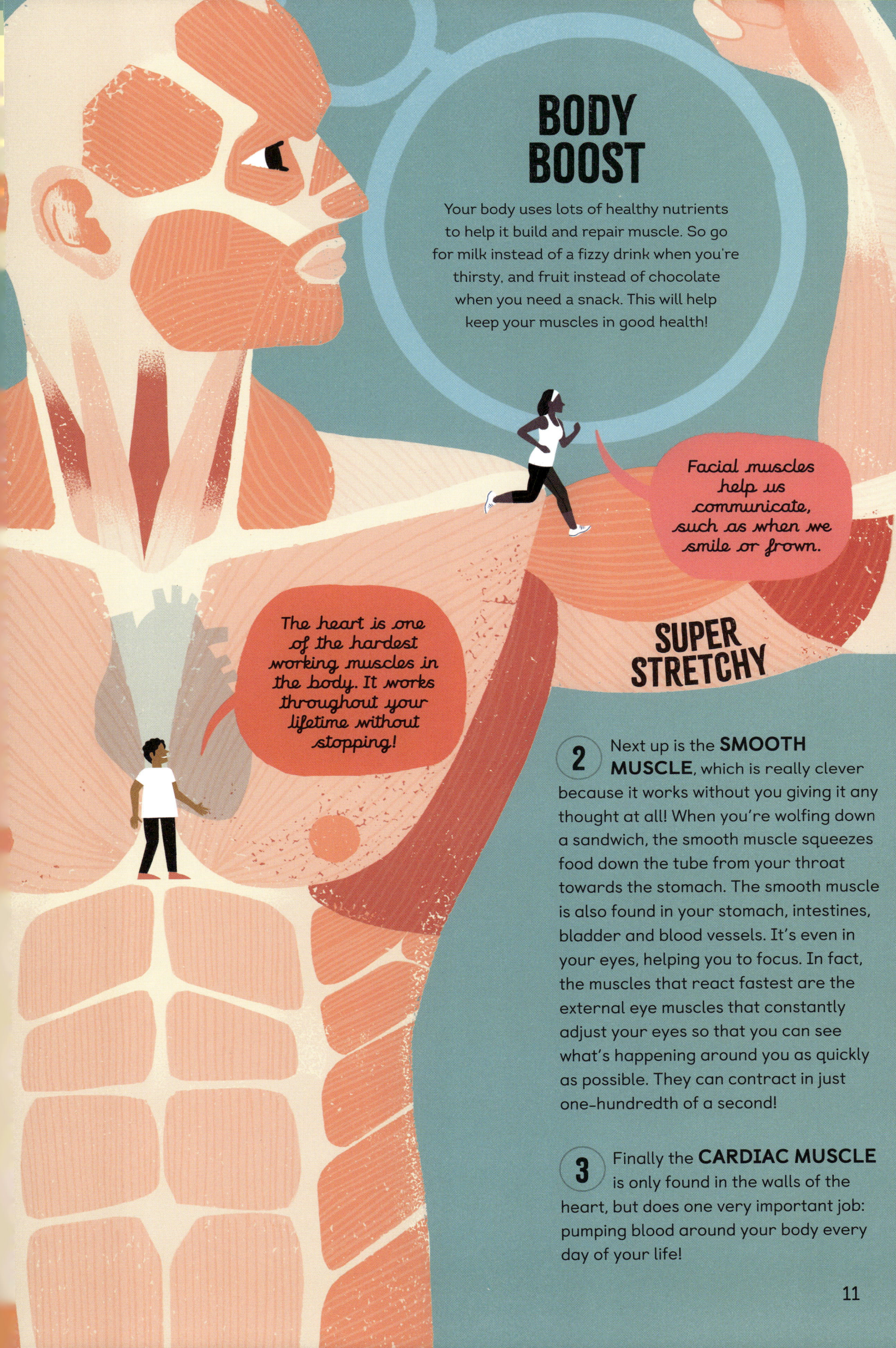

BODY BOOST

Your body uses lots of healthy nutrients to help it build and repair muscle. So go for milk instead of a fizzy drink when you're thirsty, and fruit instead of chocolate when you need a snack. This will help keep your muscles in good health!

Facial muscles help us communicate, such as when we smile or frown.

The heart is one of the hardest working muscles in the body. It works throughout your lifetime without stopping!

SUPER STRETCHY

2 Next up is the **SMOOTH MUSCLE**, which is really clever because it works without you giving it any thought at all! When you're wolfing down a sandwich, the smooth muscle squeezes food down the tube from your throat towards the stomach. The smooth muscle is also found in your stomach, intestines, bladder and blood vessels. It's even in your eyes, helping you to focus. In fact, the muscles that react fastest are the external eye muscles that constantly adjust your eyes so that you can see what's happening around you as quickly as possible. They can contract in just one-hundredth of a second!

3 Finally the **CARDIAC MUSCLE** is only found in the walls of the heart, but does one very important job: pumping blood around your body every day of your life!

THE BARE BONES

There's a song that goes, 'The hip bone's connected to the thigh bone, the thigh bone's connected to the knee bone …' and it's how we're taught at medical school. Just joking – things are a bit more complicated than that! We have a lot of bones – 206 of them in an adult body, and about 300 in a baby's body, because as we grow up, our bones fuse together.

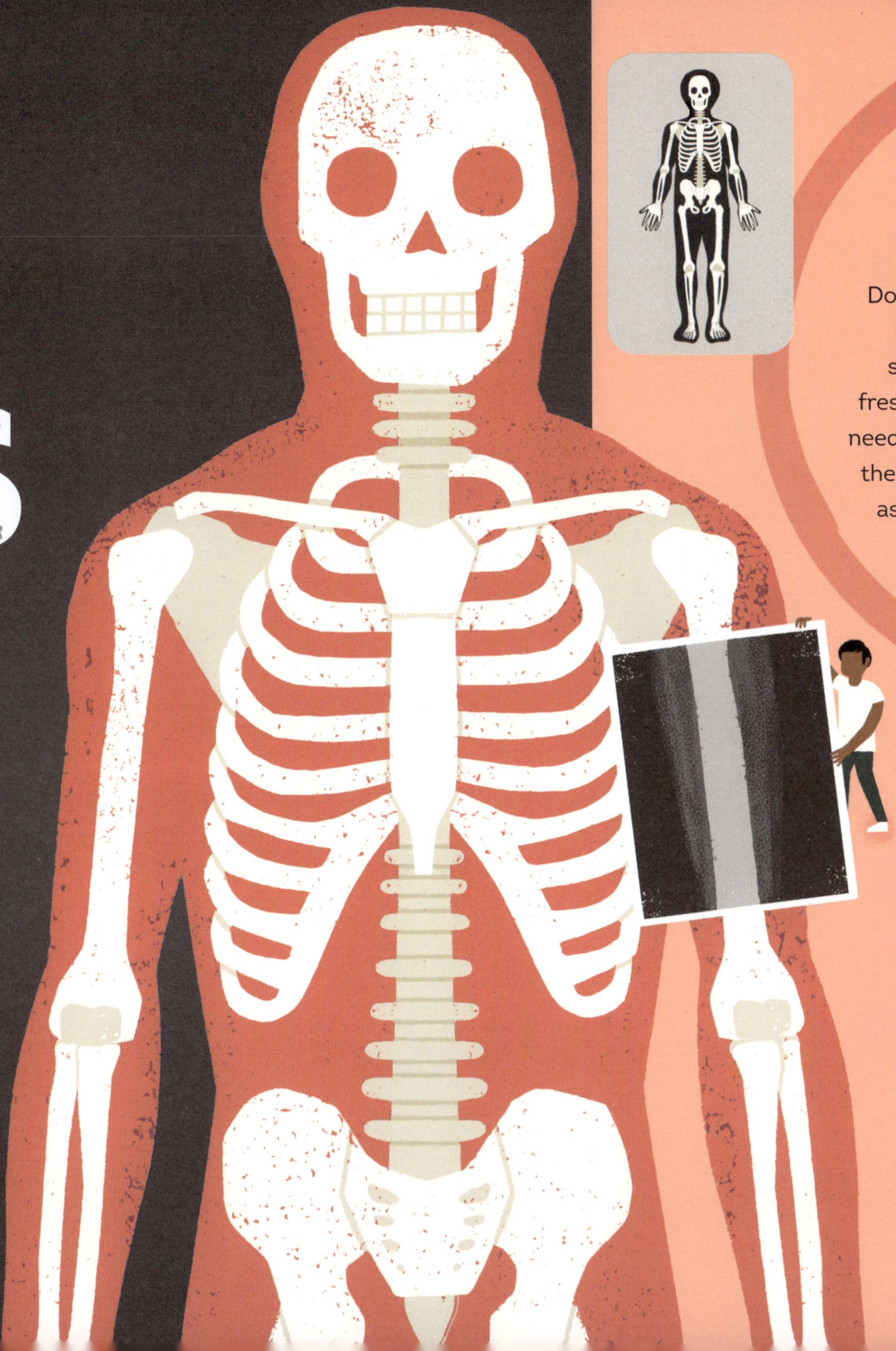

BODY BOOST

Doing plenty of exercise will build strong, healthy bones. Bones need calcium, so eat milk and cheese, almonds, and fresh vegetables such as broccoli. You also need vitamin D so that your body can absorb the calcium, which is found in oily fish such as mackerel and salmon, egg yolks, and sunlight (but don't burn your skin!).

Bones have to be strong and inflexible to hold us up, which means they don't bend very well – if they're forced, they will break. If you do break a bone, the doctor will take an X-ray, which is a special type of photograph that can see through your skin.

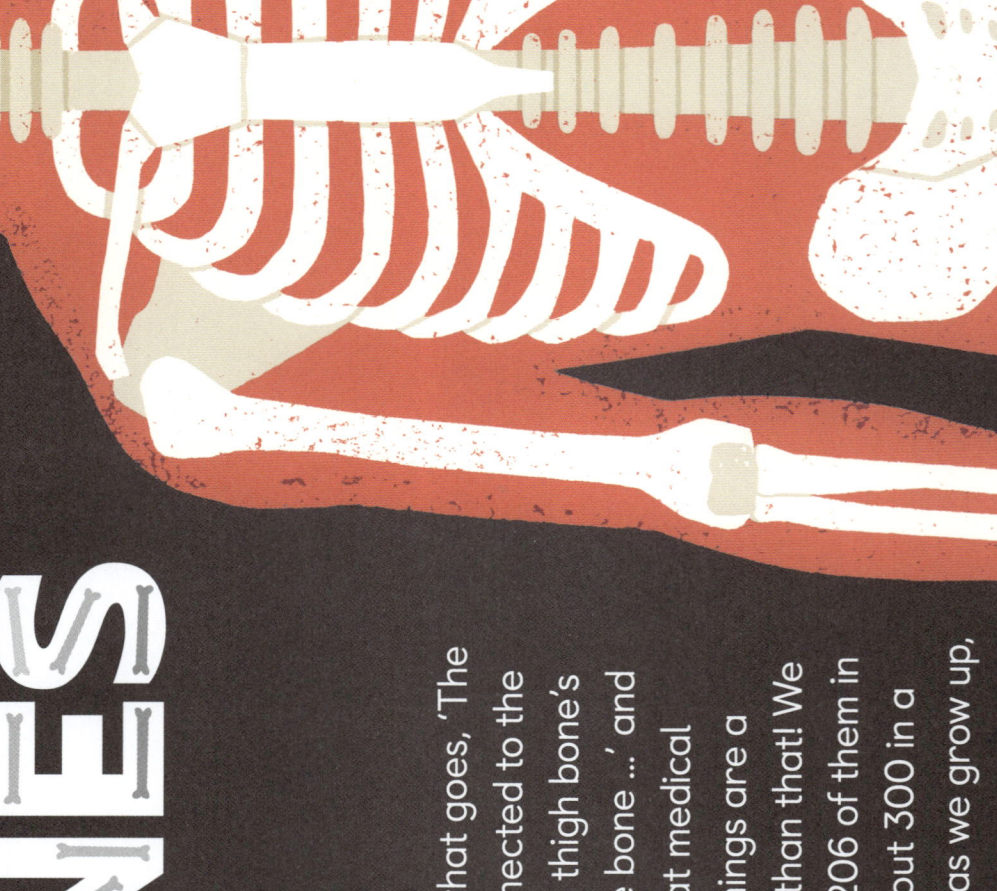

Bones are rigid organs that make up the skeleton, and they do lots of of different jobs. They're very good at protecting your insides – your skull protects your brain and your rib cage protects your heart and lungs, for example. Bones do such a good job because they're incredibly tough – per kilogram, bone is five times stronger than steel. Bones also work with your muscles to help you move, and they support your body by giving it a strong structure. Without your bones, you'd be a sort of blob!

If a bone gets broken, clever cells within the bone called osteoclasts and osteoblasts help it to heal. A doctor will often surround the damaged area with a very tough bandage called a plaster cast to protect the bone and keep it straight while it's healing.

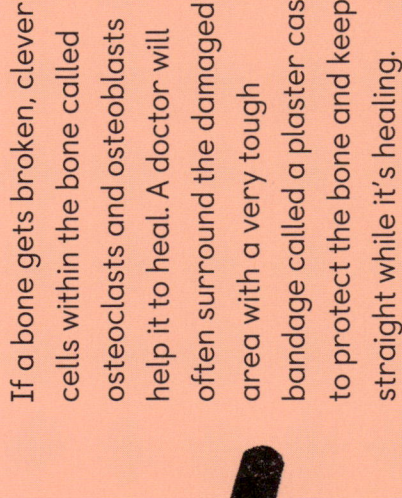

But bones aren't just thick, solid lump either! The inside of a bone has lots of small holes, a bit like a honeycomb, which makes it light as well as strong. Where two or more bones meet at a joint, a coating on their ends called cartilage protects them from crashing and grinding into each other.

Bones do less obvious jobs too, such as storing important minerals and fats that your body might need to grow and repair itself. They can even store poisons that your body can't get rid of, to lock them away safely. And, perhaps most impressively, bone marrow – a spongy tissue found deep inside large bones – is involved in making blood.

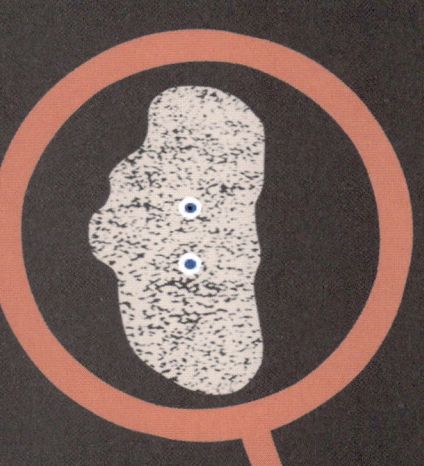

The brain and spinal cord make up the central nervous system.

Controls your muscles, so when you run, jump or laugh, this springs into action!

Receives information from your eyes to allow you to see.

Deals with touch, heat or pain. If you stub your toe the signal arrives here!

MOTOR CORTEX

SENSORY CORTEX

AUDITORY CORTEX

BROCA'S AREA
Allows you to speak and understand language.

HIPPOCAMPUS

HYPOTHALAMUS

VISUAL CORTEX

Works with your ears to help you to detect sound.

Your memories are stored here (good and bad!).

An essential but small part of the brain, this controls our need for things such as sleep and food.

CEREBELLUM

PITUITARY GLAND
Makes hormones, which are chemicals that control the body's growth and development.

The largest part of the brain, controls all the body's voluntary actions such as posture and speech.

BRAINSTEM
Also known as the medulla, controls actions you don't think about, such as breathing.

14

Up close, the human brain looks like a huge, pinky-grey-coloured walnut. But it's one of the most complex objects in the entire universe. It helps us to move, talk, recall memories and sense our surroundings. In fact, it controls almost everything the body does and is more powerful than any computer ever built!

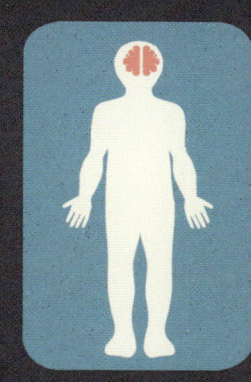

THE CONTROL CENTRE

So, let's pop up to the body's control centre for a really close look. The brain is made up of about 86 billion special nerve cells called neurons. They look like trees, with branches reaching out to connect with other neurons, allowing different parts of the brain to communicate with each other.

Weirdly, the left half of the brain controls the right side of the body, and the right side of the brain controls the left side of the body. The left half of your brain is thought to deal with emotion and creative things such as music and art, while the right half of your brain helps you to read, count and talk.

BODY BOOST

Sleep is important because it gives your body time to recover and repair. But in the night your brain will keep on working. When you dream, your brain is doing lots of things including processing all the events and information from that day. So make sure you get plenty of sleep!

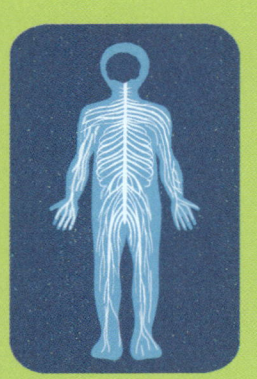

Your incredible brain has an incredibly important job – it never stops receiving and sending out information, so that you can catch a ball, work out a maths problem, or decide what to have for lunch. It's a control centre, and every control centre needs a messaging network, so that all the information has something to travel on. This network is made up of your nerves.

THE NERVE NETWORK

Nerves are made of lots of nerve cells (neurons) bundled together, just like in a cable, and they carry messages around your body. There are two main types of nerves. **SENSORY NERVES**, which gather information from your senses and take it to your brain, telling you whether a plate is hot, for example. **MOTOR NERVES** send signals from your brain to your muscles and tell them to move – maybe to move your hand away from that hot plate. This happens super quick: the fastest neurons send nerve signals at 430 kilometres per hour – faster than a racing car!

When you want to pick up your pet rabbit, for example, your brain needs to know where the rabbit is and where your hands are. Then it has to tell your hands to move towards your furry friend, and pick it up gently. Your brain manages all of this with the help of nerves.

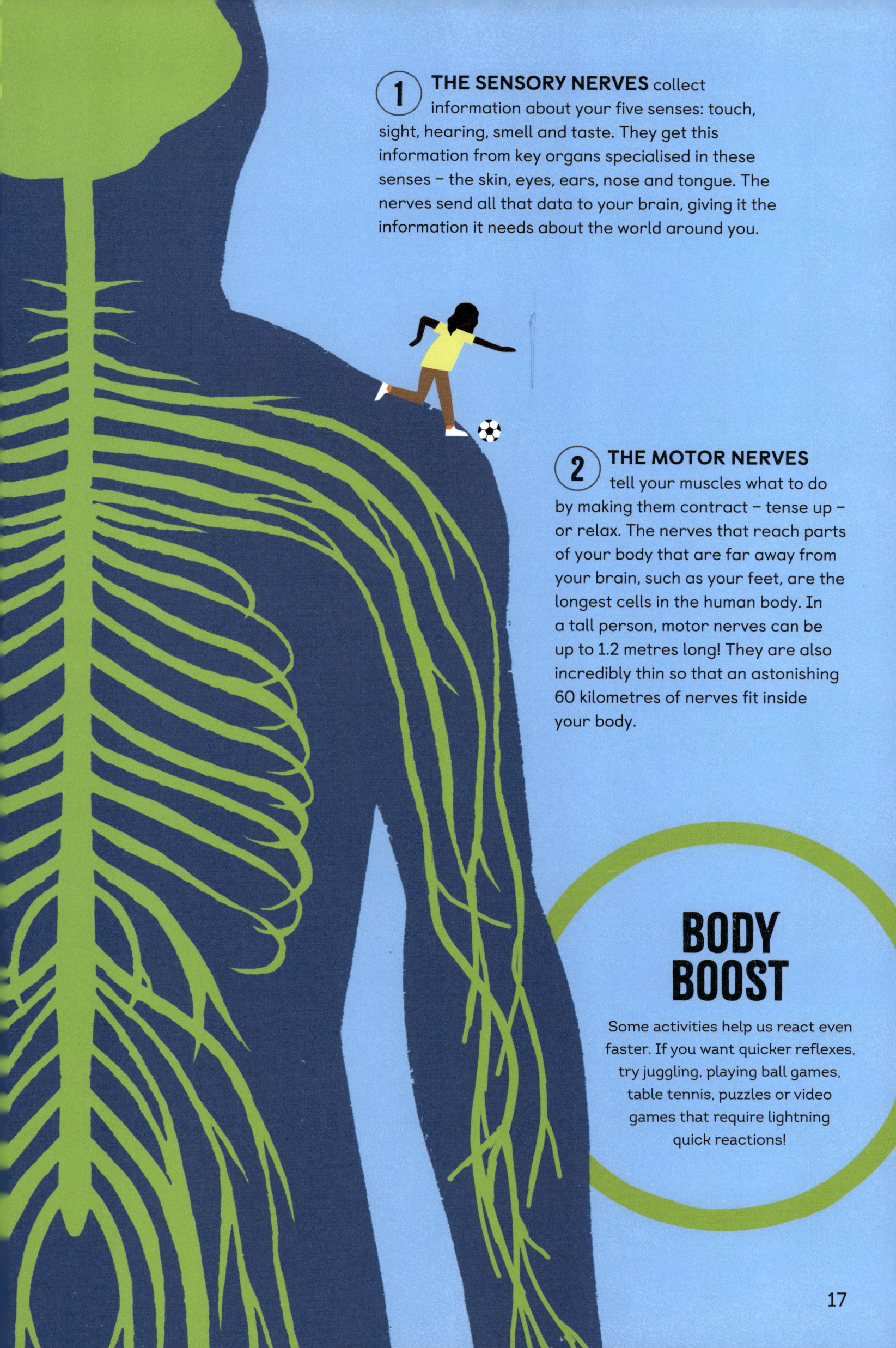

① THE SENSORY NERVES collect information about your five senses: touch, sight, hearing, smell and taste. They get this information from key organs specialised in these senses – the skin, eyes, ears, nose and tongue. The nerves send all that data to your brain, giving it the information it needs about the world around you.

② THE MOTOR NERVES tell your muscles what to do by making them contract – tense up – or relax. The nerves that reach parts of your body that are far away from your brain, such as your feet, are the longest cells in the human body. In a tall person, motor nerves can be up to 1.2 metres long! They are also incredibly thin so that an astonishing 60 kilometres of nerves fit inside your body.

BODY BOOST

Some activities help us react even faster. If you want quicker reflexes, try juggling, playing ball games, table tennis, puzzles or video games that require lightning quick reactions!

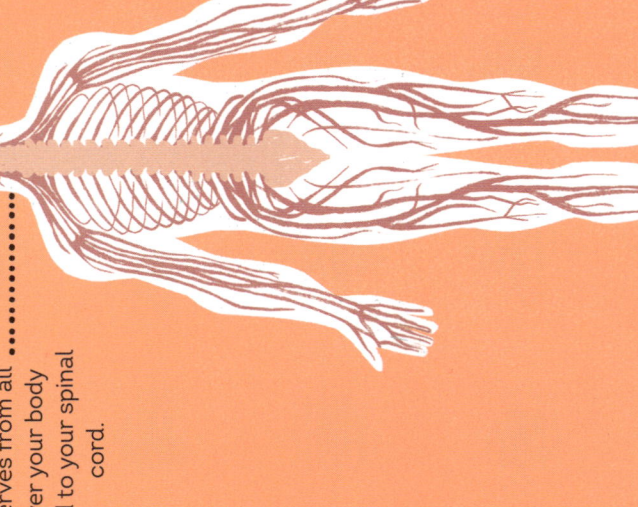

Nerves from all over your body lead to your spinal cord.

BRAIN

SPINAL CORD
The spinal cord is a bundle of nerves that passes information back and forth to the brain.

The spine needs to be strong to protect the spinal cord, but it also has to be able to move about so that you can bend your body. So, in between each vertebra there are muscles and ligaments – a tough tissue that keeps your bones in place. Together, these make sure that your spine is sturdy yet flexible. Each vertebra is also cushioned by cartilage.

VERTEBRAE
Protects the delicate spinal cord.

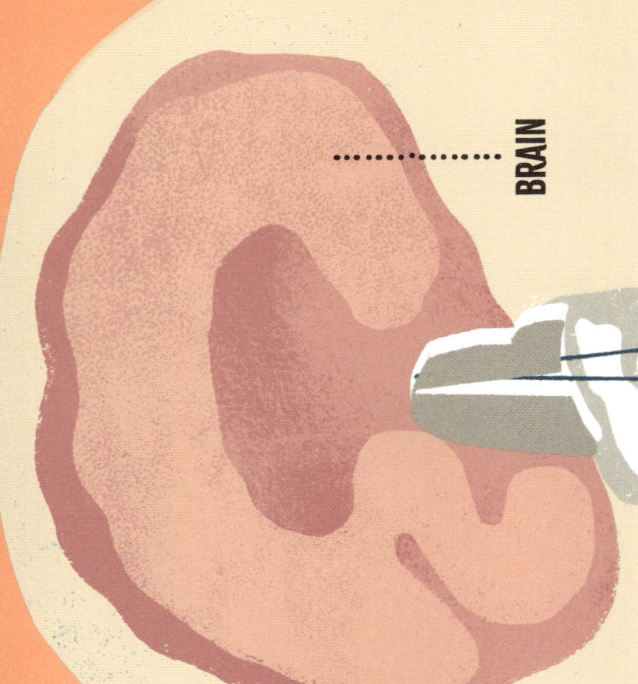

As we travelled around the brain, you might have noticed something at the base of it, dangling down like a piece of rope. This is the spinal cord. It's very delicate, so it's kept safe by 33 knobbly bones called vertebrae, which sit one on top of the other. The spinal cord runs down inside these bones, and together they make up the spine. You can feel your own spine by running your hand down your neck and back – the ridges you feel are the vertebrae.

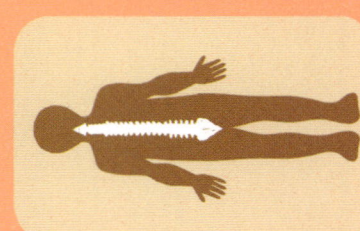

BODY BOOST

You can help keep your spine healthy by keeping active, improving your posture and making sure your back is supported when you sit down.

THE SUPER SPINE

The spinal cord is made up of a bundle of nerves about as thick as your finger. It's absolutely vital because it connects your brain to the rest of your body – information whooshes up to the brain and instructions whizz back down to the nerves to tell the muscles what to do.

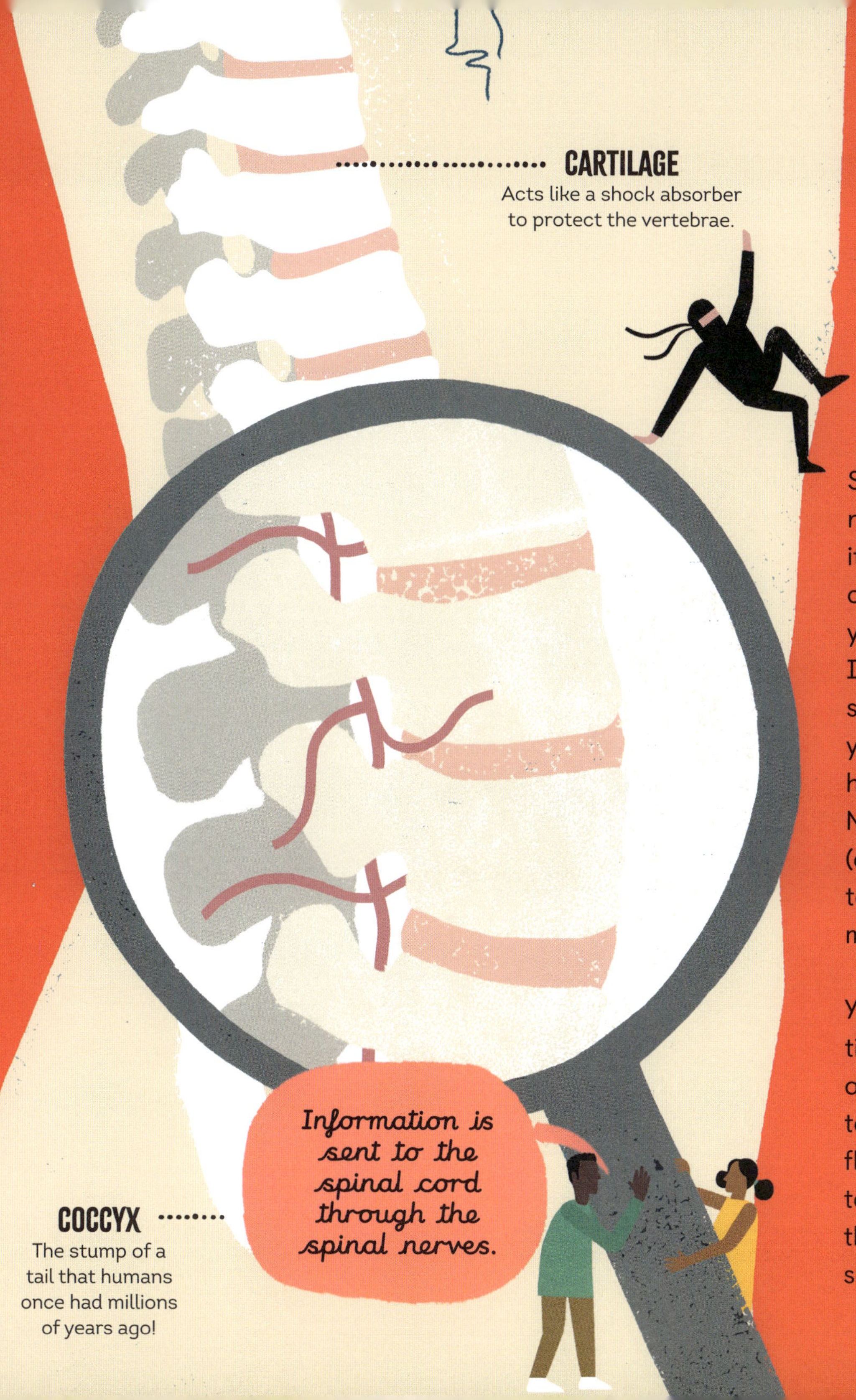

Sometimes your body needs to react to something very quickly so it can protect you. When you stand on something sharp, for example, you don't have much time to think. Instead, your body's reflexes and the spinal cord make a shortcut so that your body can react quickly without having to get your brain involved. Nerves in your foot feel the pain (ouch!) and send this information to your spinal cord, which sends a message to your foot to make it move!

Your nerves move ninja-fast all the time to keep you safe. If you trip, you automatically put out your hands to protect your body. If an insect flies towards your face, you blink to defend your eyes without even thinking. This is all thanks to your super-fast spinal cord.

CARTILAGE
Acts like a shock absorber to protect the vertebrae.

Information is sent to the spinal cord through the spinal nerves.

COCCYX
The stump of a tail that humans once had millions of years ago!

AWESOME EYES

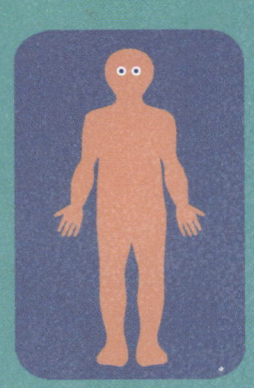

Keep your eyes peeled, because we're about to peer inside the very thing that allows us to see – the human eye. It does one of the most amazing jobs in the body, by showing us the world around us.

An adult human eye is about the size of a ping-pong ball. The skull's eye socket protects the back of the eye, while the eyelid protects the front. Glands in the corner of the eyelids produce tears, which keep the eye's surface moist, wash away things such as small specks of dirt, and help fight off germs.

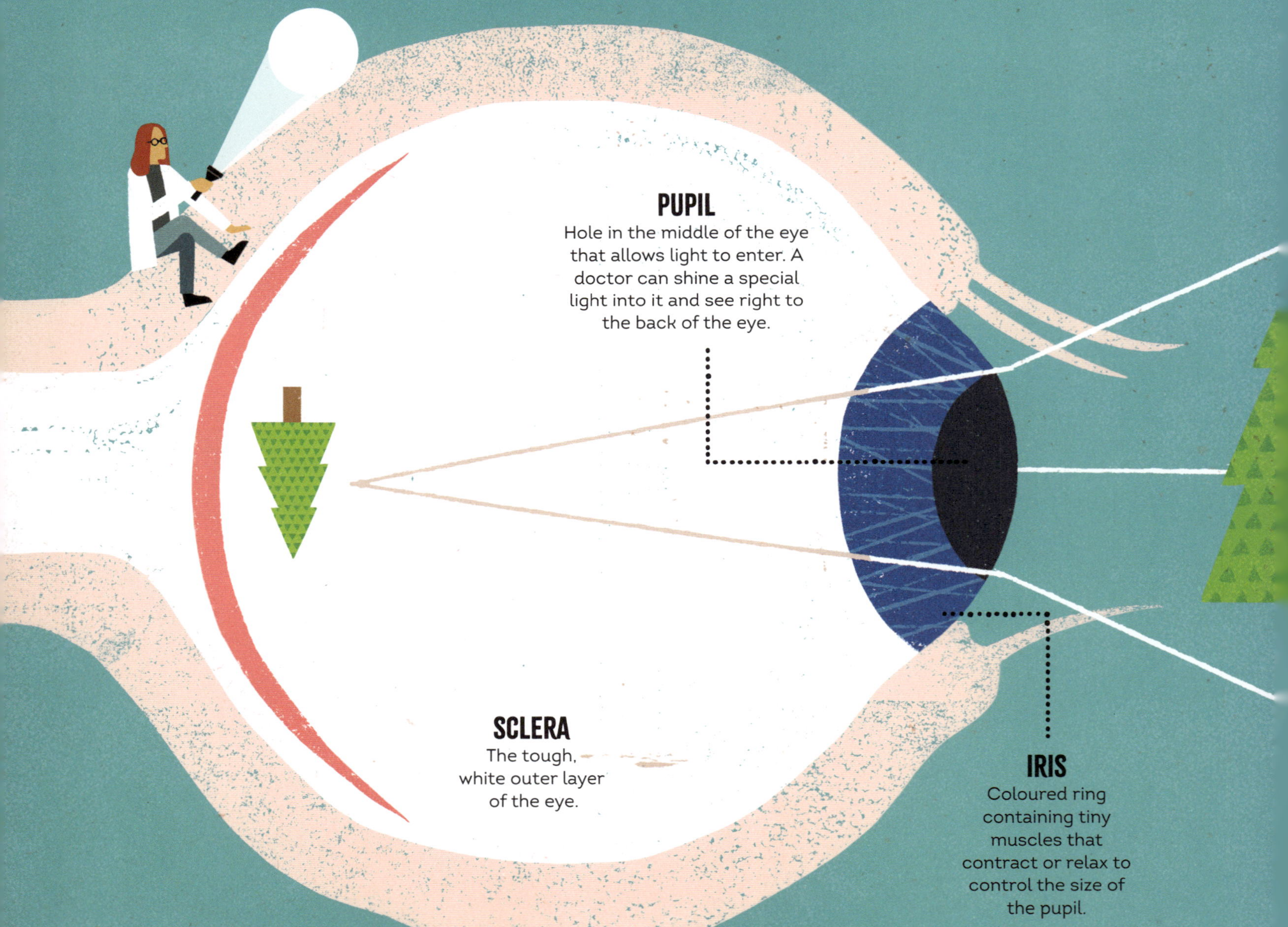

PUPIL
Hole in the middle of the eye that allows light to enter. A doctor can shine a special light into it and see right to the back of the eye.

SCLERA
The tough, white outer layer of the eye.

IRIS
Coloured ring containing tiny muscles that contract or relax to control the size of the pupil.

The eye's job is to detect light and turn it into images. When light enters through the pupil, it passes through the lens, which helps to focus the image. But the image formed on the retina, at the back of the eye, is also upside down!

There are two special cells on the retina: rods, which detect light, shapes and movement, and cones, which detect colour. The human eye can see an estimated ten million different colours, but cones need good light to work, which is why everything seems grey when there's not much light. The information gathered from the rods and cones travel to the brain along the optic nerve. The brain then turns the image the right way up so we don't have to look at an upside-down world!

The lens can change shape to help the eye focus on objects that are close up or far away. Some people's lenses don't do this properly. These short- or long-sighted people wear glasses or contact lenses to help them see.

BODY BOOST

Too much sunlight is not good for your eyes, so you should never look directly at the sun. When it's very bright, our pupils narrow to stop too much light from entering our eyes and damaging them. When it's dark, our pupils widen to allow more light to enter so we can see better.

RETINA
Retina cells turn the light into signals that are sent to the brain.

CORNEA
Delicate, transparent dome that bends light on to the lens.

LENS
Focuses light on to the retina.

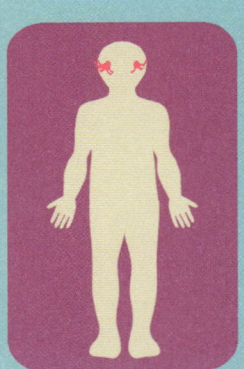

There's more to the ear than meets the eye. The bit we can see – the outer ear – is just one of three parts of the ear. The other two, the middle ear and the inner ear, are buried deep inside the skull, and we're going to crawl inside to find out more.

HELLO

In a year, the average ear makes enough wax to fill an egg cup!

HEARING HQ

EAR CANAL
Special tube inside the skull.

EARDRUM
When sound waves hit the delicate eardrum, it vibrates.

INNER EAR

COCHLEA
Vibrations from the ossicles pass into the fluid inside the cochlea, where they are picked up by tiny hairs. Sensory cells on the hairs send a signal to the brain, which we then hear.

EUSTACHIAN TUBE
The tube that connects the middle ear to the throat and back of the nasal cavity. This controls pressure within the ear.

MIDDLE EAR
There are three tiny bones here called the ossicles. They vibrate together, carrying the sound from your eardrum to the cochlea in the inner ear.

OUTER EAR

Your ears help you balance as well as hear. Next to the cochlea in the inner ear is a set of tubes called the semicircular canals that are filled with liquid. Tiny hairs inside the canals can feel the liquid swooshing around when you tilt your head, and they send this information to your brain, so it knows the position of your head and can help your body balance. There are about 15,000 hairs in the pea-sized cochlea, and all of them could fit on the head of a pin.

Your ears make sticky yellow wax, which is there to keep out water, dirt and germs, but sometimes too much gets made. When that happens, your ears can get blocked so sound waves don't reach the eardrum and sounds are muffled.

BODY BOOST

A doctor uses a special tool called an otoscope to look inside your ear canal. If you have too much wax in your ear, the doctor can carefully squirt water inside or give you drops to dissolve the wax. But you should never push anything into your ear yourself – your ear is very delicate and easily damaged.

SMELL CENTRAL

It's time to crawl up a nostril (yuck!) and discover the human body's sniffing centre. Smells tell us about the world around us, so our noses are a vital body part.

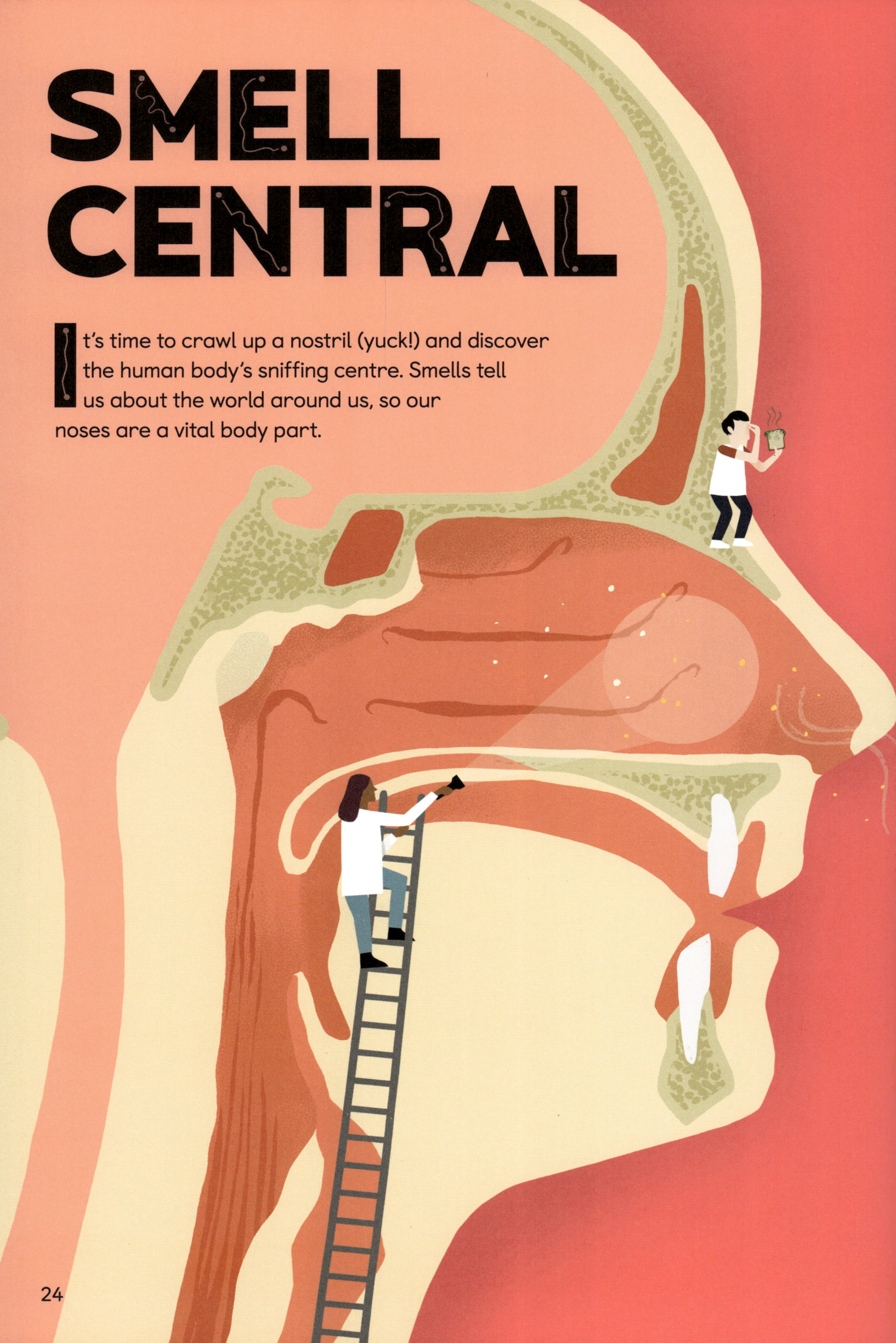

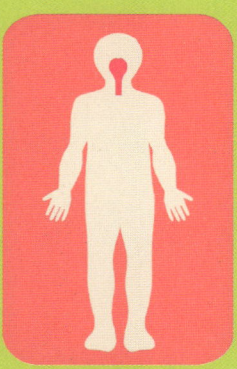

Did you know your nose protects you? Imagine you're about to gulp milk from a glass, just as you raise it to your lips you get a whiff and put it straight down. Yuck! The milk's off. Without your nose you wouldn't have found out until you'd drunk it and it made you sick. Your nose will let you know about other dangers, too – for example, if it smells dangerous gas, or smoke from a fire.

BODY BOOST

When you get a cold, your body makes lots of mucus to try and keep out the cold germs, and that's why your nose runs. If you have a cold, drink lots of water and keep warm. You might want to also study your snot, as it can be all sorts of colours, which can mean different things – but not all of them health related!

GREEN OR YELLOW
Green or yellow snot – often means you have an infection, because of the colour of the cells the body makes to fight infection.

Your nose also helps you breathe. And as you're breathing through it, your nose acts as a special air filter by making a sticky fluid called mucus (or snot), which traps dust and germs. Snot sometimes dries up and becomes a bogey.

BROWN OR RED
Brown or red snot – your nose's fragile blood vessels might have been damaged by too much blowing or picking.

DARK GREY
Dark grey snot – your nose probably has trapped dust or dirt in it.

Particular smells often trigger memories.

If we travel high up to the back of the nose we'll find a special patch of very sensitive nerves. When the cells here detect a smell they send signals to the brain, which then tries to identify what the smell is. The nose can detect an estimated one trillion different smells!

Taste and smell are closely linked because the back of the nose opens into the back of the mouth. When you eat, food smells waft up to your nose. A smell is made up of a few incredibly tiny particles of whatever's being smelt. These particles float about, so when you sniff a flower, tiny parts of the flower are going up your nose. And when you sniff dog poo, tiny bits of poo are going up your nose – don't worry, it sounds horrible but it won't harm you!

Brush your teeth gently for two minutes twice a day

ENAMEL
Makes the teeth hard for biting, and protects the dentine. Enamel has no nerves or feeling in it.

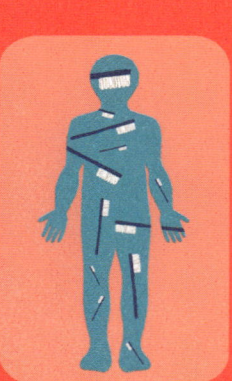

PULP
Contains nerves and blood vessels.

CHOMPING TEETH

Your teeth are so important. Without them, you wouldn't be able to crunch on vegetables or bite into toast. Let's examine a set – but be careful not to get nibbled …

Teeth are designed to break up food in to small pieces and mix it with saliva (spit). This is the beginning of the process of digestion – how our bodies break down the food we eat and use its energy to grow and repair itself. We have four main types of teeth, well designed for the jobs they need to do.

ROOT
Fixes the tooth to the jaw and helps it stay in place.

26

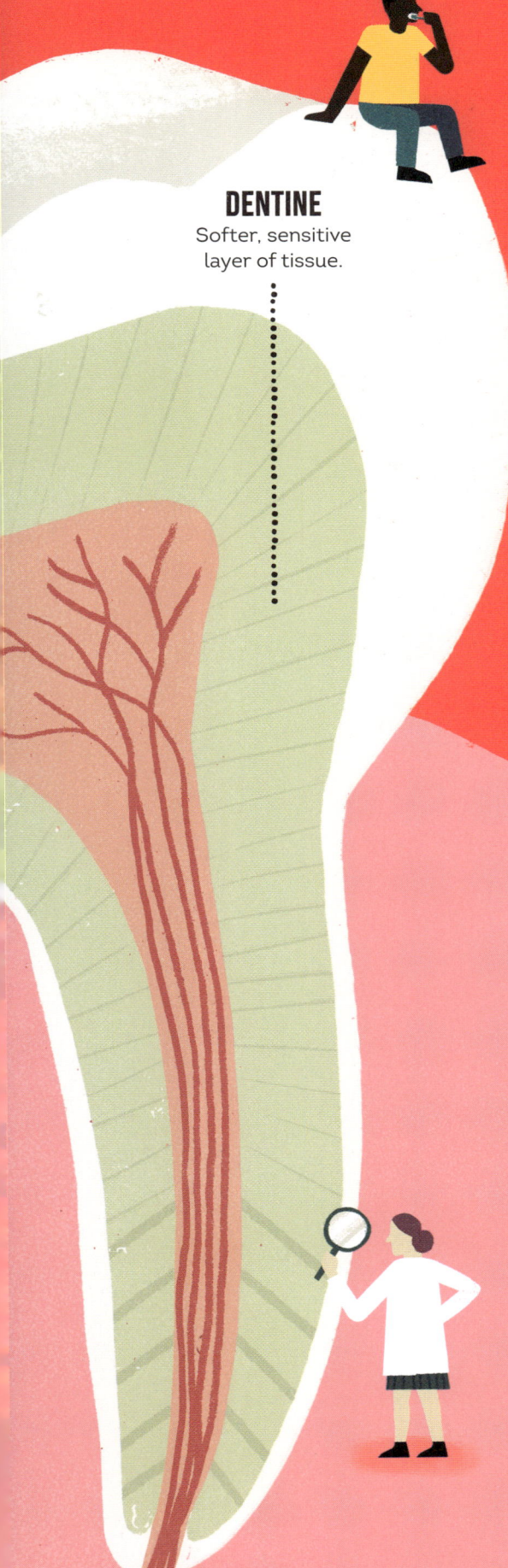

DENTINE
Softer, sensitive layer of tissue.

BODY BOOST

You might like sweets, but your teeth definitely don't! The germs living in your mouth use sugar to grow and then attack the enamel, decaying it, exposing the dentine underneath and giving you toothache. Brushing your teeth twice a day helps to remove bits of food and germs that can harm them, and going to the dentist regularly means any problems can be spotted before they get too serious.

Our teeth begin to grow before we are born but it takes until we are about six months old before our first set, called milk teeth, start to become visible. They grow through tissue called gums, which are part of the lining of our mouths, and seal the teeth in place. Later, when we're about six years old, bigger teeth grow and start to push the milk teeth out. You can sometimes see the new tooth underneath when a milk tooth comes out.

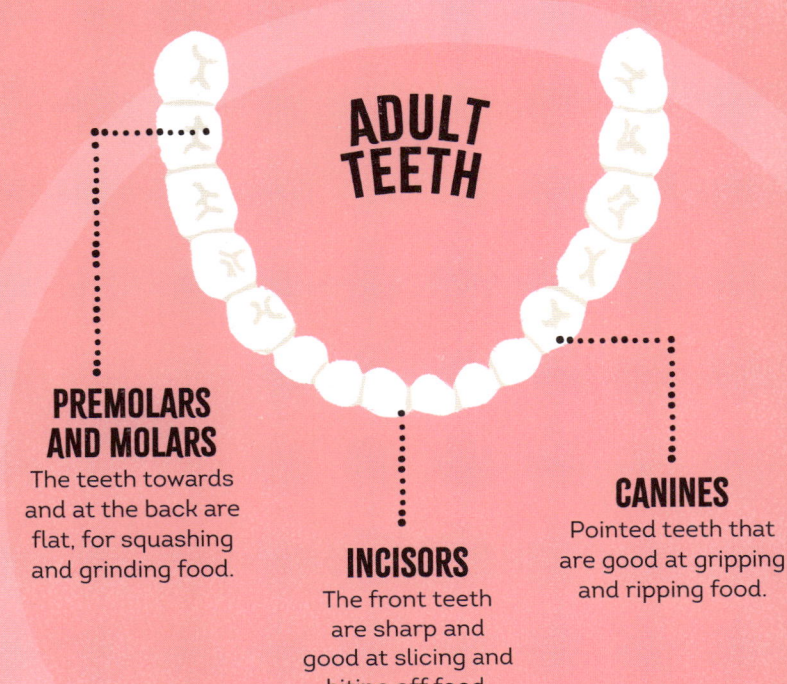

ADULT TEETH

PREMOLARS AND MOLARS
The teeth towards and at the back are flat, for squashing and grinding food.

INCISORS
The front teeth are sharp and good at slicing and biting off food.

CANINES
Pointed teeth that are good at gripping and ripping food.

Once we're grown up, four new teeth grow – on the top and bottom of the back of our mouth. These are called wisdom teeth, although they don't make you clever. No one really knows why they grow – it might be because our ancestors would have needed new grinding teeth to replace worn-out ones.

27

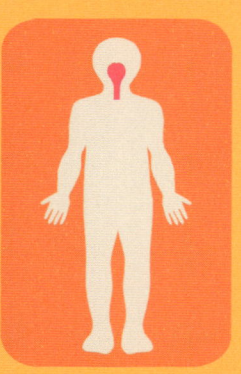

While you're tucking into a delicious plate of spaghetti, your mouth is hard at work. Altogether, it takes between 24 and 72 hours for food to travel down to your stomach, through your intestines and finally out of your body. And the first stop on that long journey is your mouth.

MOUTH MATTERS

Let's watch a mouth in action. As your teeth chew, your mouth releases saliva. This makes food slippery so it can be swallowed easily. Saliva contains special chemicals called enzymes, which help to break down food so that it can be absorbed more easily in the stomach.

As you chew, your tongue tastes the food using taste buds that are found in tiny bumps, called papillae, on the surface of your tongue. There are about 10,000 of these special taste sensors, and they give the brain information on what is being eaten. Your taste buds can identify five main tastes: sweet, sour, salty, bitter and umami (a savoury flavour).

BODY BOOST

Eating fast can make you feel too full, because it takes a while for the full-up message to arrive in your brain. Try to avoid eating in front of a screen, because we eat much more quickly when we're distracted and might end up eating too much.

The tube that carries chewed-up food into your stomach is called the oesophagus. When you swallow, the tongue pushes the food to the back of the throat. The nerves in the back of the throat sense the food and tell the brain. The brain then tells the smooth muscle in the oesophagus to start contracting. This squeezes the food down, like someone pushing toothpaste through a tube.

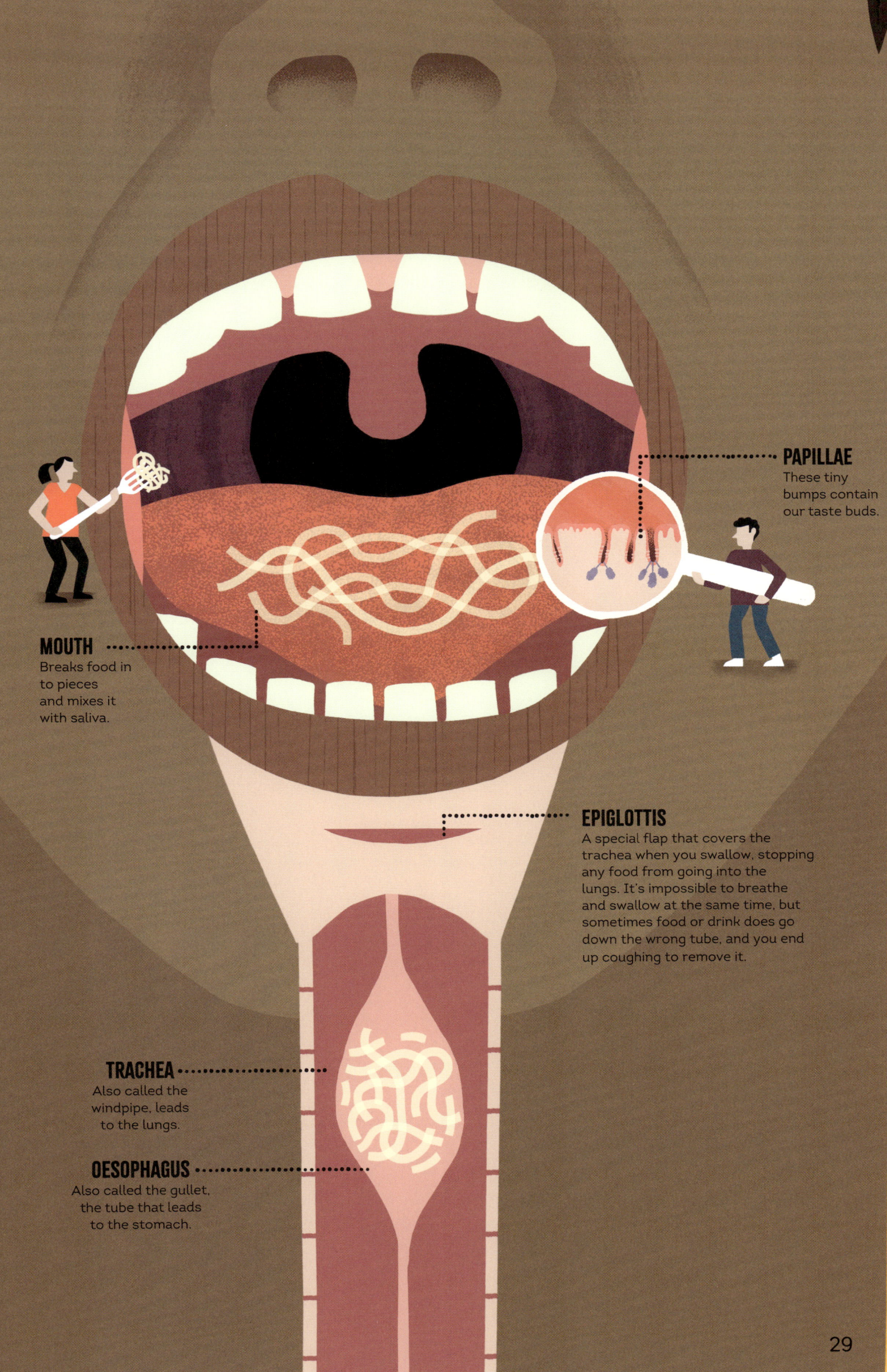

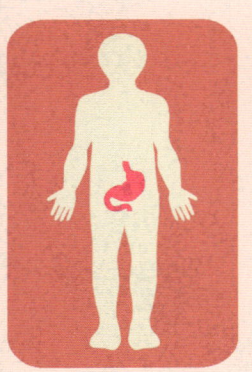

OK, so your spaghetti has been chewed up by your teeth, mixed with saliva in your mouth, and pushed down a tube into your stomach. It's already in small, mushy pieces, but the stomach is where it gets broken down even more so that all the goodness can be released from the food. Your spaghetti turns in to a sort of soup, which is easy for your body to absorb and digest.

SOUPED UP

Let's continue our microscopic journey inside the stomach. But how do we get there? If you thought the stomach was near the belly button, you'd be way off course. It's higher up, just below the breastbone on the left-hand side of the chest.

SQUEEZE

INTESTINE

BODY BOOST

If you eat too much sugary food, your pancreas can get tired from having to release so much insulin, and so the cells in your body stop responding to it. This is called type 2 diabetes, and people with it have to take medication for the rest of their lives. That's why it's important not to eat too much sugar.

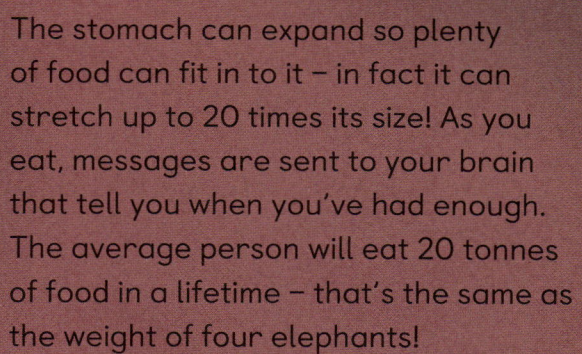

The stomach can expand so plenty of food can fit in to it – in fact it can stretch up to 20 times its size! As you eat, messages are sent to your brain that tell you when you've had enough. The average person will eat 20 tonnes of food in a lifetime – that's the same as the weight of four elephants!

STRETCH

STOMACH

Now we're inside, we can see the stomach is like a stretchy sack. Muscles squeeze and relax to help mix food and stomach acid together, making gloopy soup. Since stomach acid is strong enough to dissolve food, a thick protective layer of mucus coats the stomach lining. Even so, about one million stomach cells are killed every minute, replaced just as quickly by the hard-working body. Once the food has turned into soup, the stomach muscles push it into the intestines.

PANCREAS

The pancreas is a small, squashy organ that sits behind your stomach and produces special enzymes that break down food. It also controls the level of sugar in your blood. When sugar from digested food enters your bloodstream, the pancreas releases a chemical called insulin. This tells all the cells in your body to store excess sugar, so that the amount of sugar in your body is kept stable. However, people with type 1 diabetes have a pancreas that doesn't work properly, so they have to inject man-made insulin into their bloodstream when they eat.

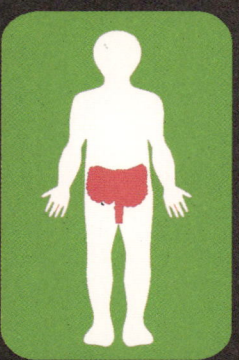

Get ready for a gut-churning trip through the intestines! It's their job to absorb the goodness from the food we eat. The intestines are a continuous tube, starting below your stomach and ending at your anus, which is the scientific term for the opening in your bottom.

A LOT OF GUTS

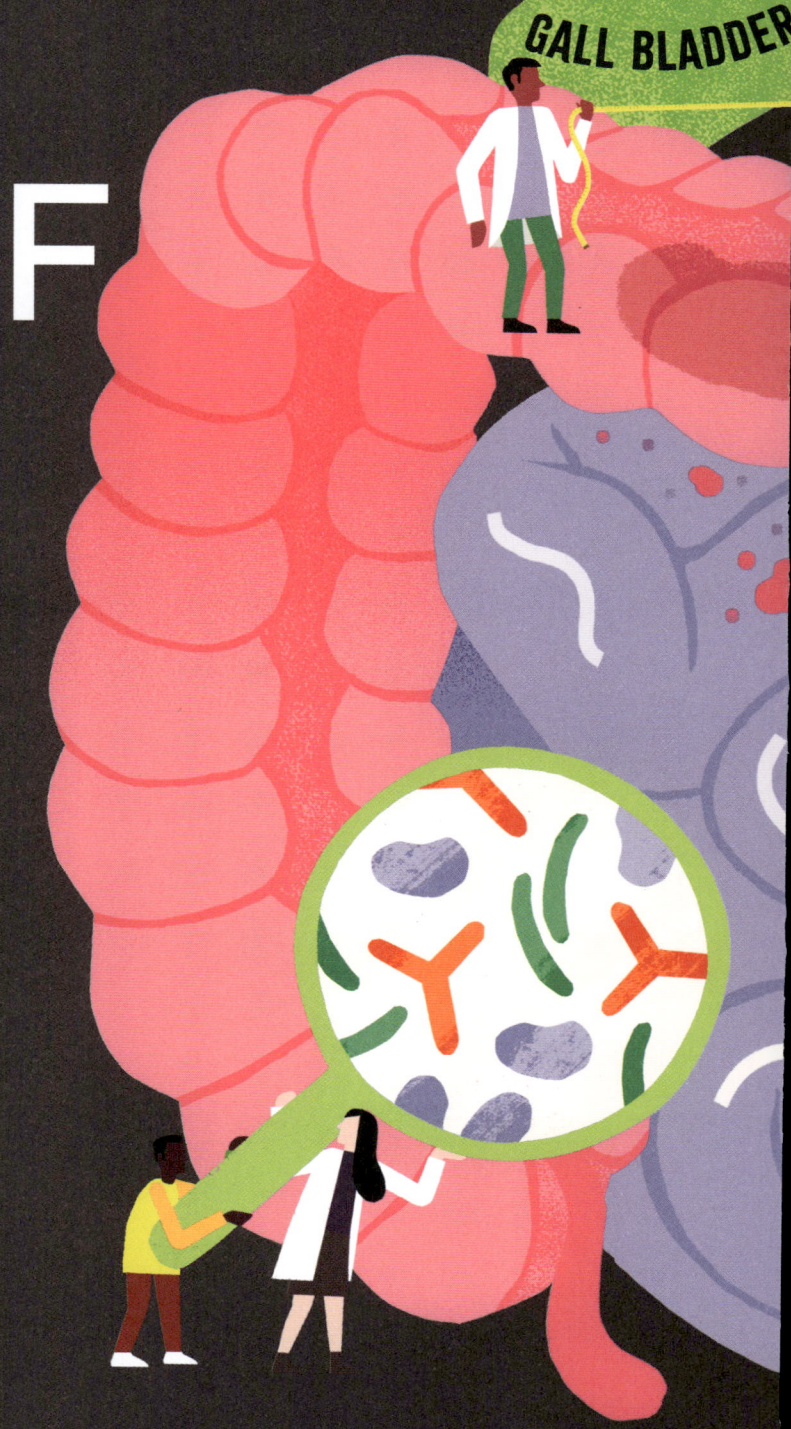

Intestines come in two parts, the small and the large intestines. The small intestine is where most of digestion happens. In an adult, it measures about 5 metres long – that's about the same as the height of a double-decker bus! It fits because it's tightly coiled in to the space beneath our stomach.

Enzymes are released from the pancreas into the intestines when food is detected. As the food moves through the small intestine, it's broken down in to tiny pieces that are easily absorbed in to the bloodstream. Bacteria in the intestine also helps to break up food, releasing gas at the same time, which is why people fart. Interesting fact: the average person passes enough wind to fill a party balloon each day!

It usually takes about 16 hours for the digesting food to pass through the large intestine. By the end of the journey, a lot of the water and all the good, nutritious stuff from the food has been absorbed into the body. The body doesn't need what's left – the poo!

GALL BLADDER

A small, hard-working organ just below the liver. It stores bile, a substance made in the liver and released by the gall bladder into the intestines. Like washing-up liquid, it helps break down fats in partly digested food.

BODY BOOST

Poo varies in shape and size depending on lots of things. If you're unwell, you might have diarrhoea – runny poo caused by the body trying to flush out an infection. At other times, poo might be difficult to release – this is called constipation, and is sometimes caused by not drinking enough water, or eating enough vegetables.

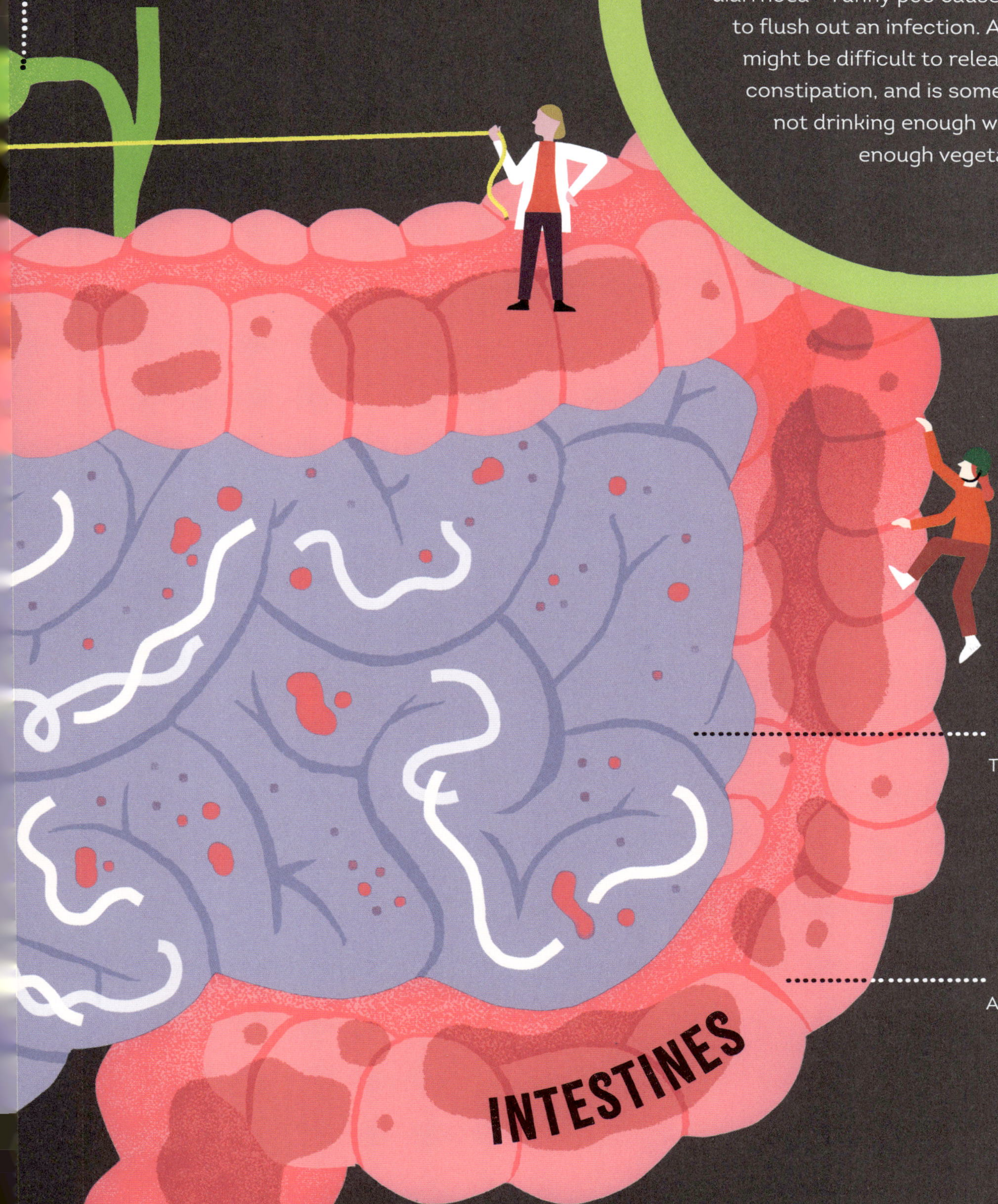

SMALL INTESTINE

This is where most of the digestion happens.

LARGE INTESTINE

After the small intestines, food passes into the large intestines.

INTESTINES

We store poo in the lower part of the large intestine until we go to the toilet and let it out. Poo is full of waste, as well as germs or chemicals that it wants to get rid of. It's really important to wash your hands after going to the toilet so that all the harmful germs are washed away.

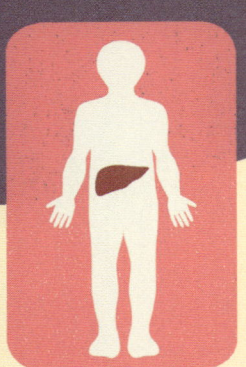

The next stop on our marvellous adventure is to visit the liver, the human body's largest internal organ. The liver does over 500 different jobs, and is one of the hardest working organs in the body. It's so amazing that it can repair itself and even regrow!

THE MIRACULOUS LIVER

First we have to get there. The liver is on the right-hand side of the body. It's a wedge-shaped organ that sits next to the stomach, protected by the lower part of the ribs.

Once we're in the liver, there's lots going on! All those nutrients that were absorbed by your intestines are carried here by a large vein, and the liver gets to work on them. It breaks down sugars to give the body energy, and insulin from the pancreas tells it to store any extra sugar until it's needed. At the same time, the liver makes the bile stored in the gall bladder, which helps to break down fat.

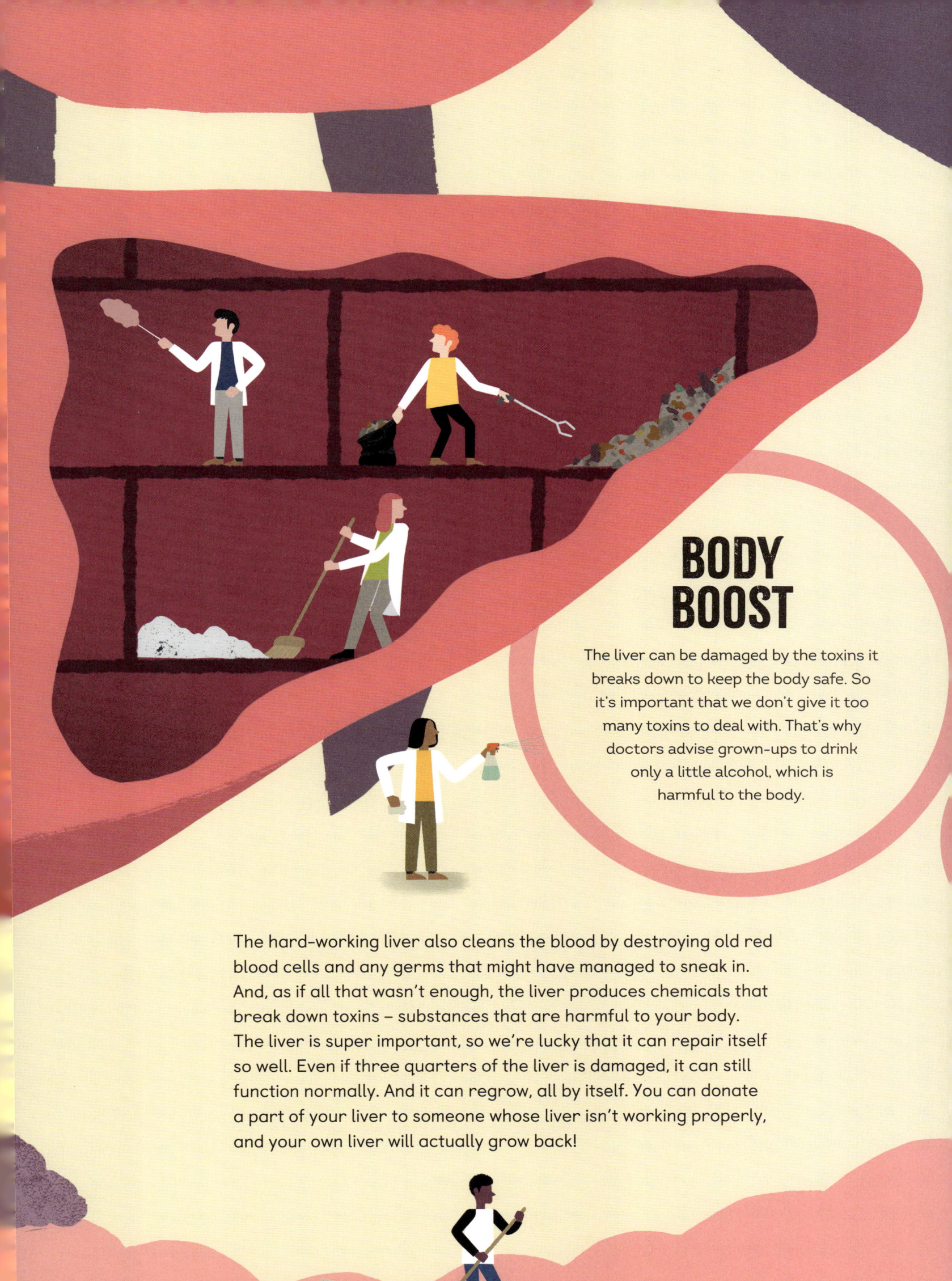

BODY BOOST

The liver can be damaged by the toxins it breaks down to keep the body safe. So it's important that we don't give it too many toxins to deal with. That's why doctors advise grown-ups to drink only a little alcohol, which is harmful to the body.

The hard-working liver also cleans the blood by destroying old red blood cells and any germs that might have managed to sneak in. And, as if all that wasn't enough, the liver produces chemicals that break down toxins – substances that are harmful to your body. The liver is super important, so we're lucky that it can repair itself so well. Even if three quarters of the liver is damaged, it can still function normally. And it can regrow, all by itself. You can donate a part of your liver to someone whose liver isn't working properly, and your own liver will actually grow back!

THE CLEAN-UP TEAM

RENAL VEIN
Carries away blood filtered by the kidney.

RENAL ARTERY
Carries blood from the heart to the kidney.

KIDNEY
We have two kidneys, one on each side of the body, just below the lowest rib.

URETER
This tube takes the urine to be stored in the bladder.

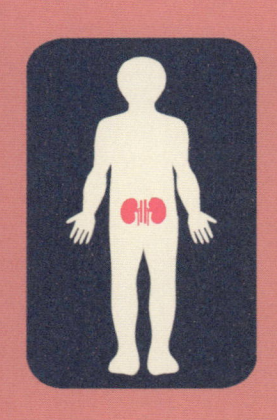

You might not give too much thought to your kidneys, but they're your body's cleaners, and without them you wouldn't be alive. So let's give a big high-five to our kidneys as we take a closer look.

The kidneys are shaped like kidney beans. They're there to deal with the waste products the body's cells don't need any more. If this waste was left in the blood, it could poison the body. So the kidneys filter the blood and sort the waste from the things that the body wants to keep, such as red blood cells or oxygen.

36

The filtering happens in units called nephrons. Each kidney has about a million nephrons, which allow waste products and excess water to pass from the blood and be turned into urine (wee). At the same time, the nephrons keep important cells and nutrients in the bloodstream. Cleverly, as the blood is filtered, the nephrons are able to catch and put back any chemicals that accidentally leak out but the body needs.

BODY BOOST

It's vital to your kidneys that you have enough to drink. When you haven't drunk enough, your urine is very concentrated and looks dark yellow. When you've had a lot to drink, it can be very light yellow or almost clear. The best colour is a light yellow – not too dark and not too light.

NEPHRON
The kidney's filtering unit. There are millions of these.

RENAL PELVIS
Funnels the urine into the ureter.

RENAL PYRAMID
These triangle-shaped sections carry urine from the outer part of the kidney towards the ureter.

We need water to flush the kidneys and help them do their job. How much we should drink varies depending on what we've been doing. For example, if it's hot and we've been sweating, then we'll need more water because we've lost some in the sweat. But we don't just get water from the tap – fruits and vegetables also have plenty of water in them (as well as lots of good nutrients, which is yet another reason to eat fruit and veg)!

Without our kidneys, waste products would quickly build up in our blood to toxic levels. If someone's kidneys aren't working properly, their blood might have to be passed through a machine in a process called kidney dialysis, which is an artificial way to filter the blood.

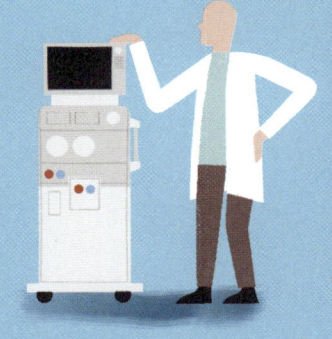

37

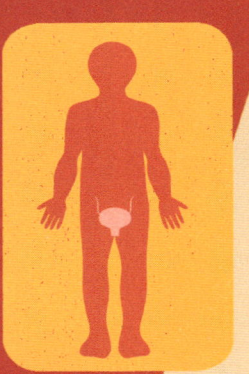

All that wee produced by the kidneys collects in the bladder. Although the bladder's job sounds simple enough, the ability to hold and get rid of urine is actually a remarkable piece of engineering.

THE AMAZING ELASTIC BLADDER

Hold your nose, because inside the bladder there's lots of strong-smelling wee sloshing about! The bladder is a bit like a balloon because it can stretch to many times its original size thanks to a special, elastic type of cell that lines the bladder wall. The bladder usually holds about 350 millilitres of urine, but it can hold approximately an astonishing 500 millilitres!

The base of the bladder is surrounded by pelvic-floor muscles, which help to keep things watertight until you want to have a wee. As your bladder fills, nerves in its wall sense it stretching and relay this information to your brain. When the bladder is about 50 per cent full, the nerves trigger the urge to wee. As your bladder continues to fill, the signal from the nerves gets stronger and is harder to ignore.

You probably don't think twice about having a wee, but passing urine is a very carefully coordinated event. A special layer of muscle that surrounds the bladder, known as the detrusor muscle, contracts and squeezes the bladder. At the same time, the pelvic-floor muscles relax. This allows urine to be squeezed out of your bladder through a tube called the urethra.

BODY BOOST

Sometimes people don't make it to the toilet in time. This is embarrassing but quite common. The muscle in the bladder can get over-excited and squeezes when it's not supposed to, so that urine is pushed out. When someone's asleep, the muscle can get confused and squeeze, so that they wet the bed. If this happens often, a doctor can help the person to train their bladder so that it knows when to release and when not to.

URETER
The tube leading from the kidney.

Time to go to the toilet!

URINE

PELVIC-FLOOR MUSCLES

BLADDER
Where wee is stored.

URETHRA
The tube that carries urine, or wee, from the body.

W.C.

THE THUMPING HEART

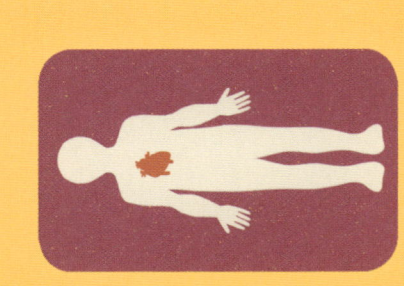

Hold out your closed fist – that's roughly how big your heart is. Your thumping heart is the main organ in your circulatory system, and it's made of cardiac muscle. It's one big pump, sending blood around the body so that all its cells get the fresh supply of oxygen-rich blood that they need to survive.

You'll see that the heart has four chambers: two on the right and two on the left. Valves at the entrance of each chamber prevent the blood from going the wrong way.

A single heartbeat is actually the heart muscle contracting to pump the blood. It takes about a minute for blood to make one journey around your body. The heart works very hard – in one day, it pumps the blood a distance of nineteen thousand kilometres around your body, and it does this without ever taking a break.

Quick! Hold on to something that floats, because we're about to be swooshed through the bloodstream along a vein towards the heart, which is the next step on our marvellous adventure.

1. Blood that has been around the body enters the heart on the right side, through a large vein called the vena cava.

4. The pulmonary artery carries the blood to the lungs, to pick up oxygen from the alveoli.

5. The pulmonary vein brings the oxygen-rich blood back to the heart.

8. The aorta and other arteries carry the oxygen-rich blood to all the body's cells.

BODY BOOST

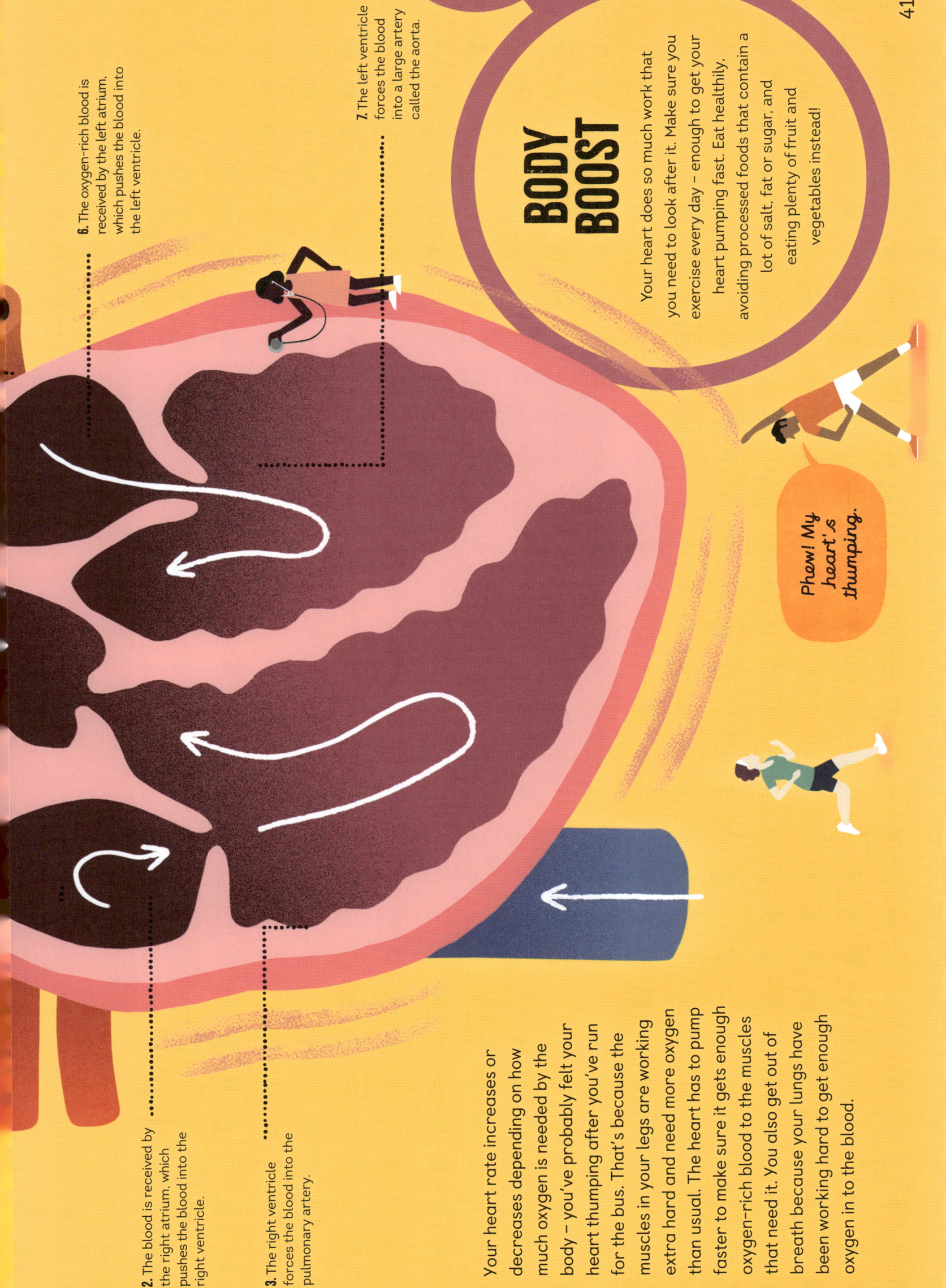

Your heart does so much work that you need to look after it. Make sure you exercise every day – enough to get your heart pumping fast. Eat healthily, avoiding processed foods that contain a lot of salt, fat or sugar, and eating plenty of fruit and vegetables instead!

Phew! My heart's thumping.

2. The blood is received by the right atrium, which pushes the blood into the right ventricle.

3. The right ventricle forces the blood into the pulmonary artery.

6. The oxygen-rich blood is received by the left atrium, which pushes the blood into the left ventricle.

7. The left ventricle forces the blood into a large artery called the aorta.

Your heart rate increases or decreases depending on how much oxygen is needed by the body – you've probably felt your heart thumping after you've run for the bus. That's because the muscles in your legs are working extra hard and need more oxygen than usual. The heart has to pump faster to make sure it gets enough oxygen-rich blood to the muscles that need it. You also get out of breath because your lungs have been working hard to get enough oxygen in to the blood.

41

THE INFLATABLE LUNGS

Your lungs never stop moving, from the second you're born to your very last breath. Let's take a closer look at these incredible organs.

The lungs are big spongy sacks that sit on top of a thick sheet of muscle called the diaphragm. The diaphragm is pulled down when you breathe in, allowing the chest wall to move outwards and air to be sucked in through the mouth and nose into the lungs. When the diaphragm relaxes, the opposite happens: the lungs are squeezed and air leaves as you breathe out.

The point of breathing is to do two important jobs. First, to transfer oxygen from the air into your bloodstream, because the cells in your body need oxygen to survive. And second, to get rid of carbon dioxide. Your body's cells make this gas as they use energy, and your lungs remove it from your blood, releasing it back into the air.

BRONCHIOLES

BRONCHUS
The trachea splits in to two pipes (the bronchi), which lead to each lung.

DIAPHRAGM
Thick sheet of muscle that sits on the bottom of the lungs.

TRACHEA
Leads from the mouth down into the lungs (also called the windpipe).

BODY BOOST
Some people suffer from asthma and so sometimes the tubes in their lungs become sensitive and swell, making it difficult to breathe. This can be treated with medicine in an inhaler. It's important to exercise – whether you have asthma or not – to improve how well your lungs work.

The thin membrane that covers our lungs is called the pleura.

BRONCHUS
Here is the second bronchus that leads to the right-hand lung.

Small cells line the lungs and the trachea (the windpipe). They are covered in microscopic hair-lilke structures, which protect the body from germs.

Watch out, because here comes a germ now! The hairs wiggle the germ, trapped in mucus, up the trachea towards the throat. Then the germ is swallowed, and is killed by stomach acid. If germs or dust irritate the trachea and the lungs, we cough to get rid of them.

BRONCHIOLES
The bronchi divide within the lungs in to bronchioles. Then they divide again and again, getting smaller and smaller. There are more than 2,400 kilometres of tubes in your lungs!

ALVEOLI
Inside these tiny sacs, oxygen transfers into the blood, and carbon dioxide is removed. The blood vessels surrounding the alveoli transport the oxygen-rich blood to the heart, where it is pumped around the body.

TINY TUBES

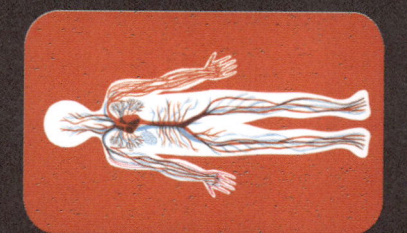

We're going back to the bloodstream for the next bit of our human body adventure, but this time we're travelling all over the body in blood vessels, which are the tubes that carry blood. An adult has up to 100,000 kilometres of blood vessels – that's enough to stretch around the world two and a half times!

CAPILLARIES have very thing walls and release the oxygen and nutrients being carried by the blood to your cells. Waste products also leave the cells and enter the capillaries where they are absorbed by the blood, which then makes its way back to the heart.

VEINS carry blood back to the heart from the rest of the body. This is a difficult job, especially down at the bottom of your legs. It's a long way back to the heart, and if you're standing or sitting up, gravity is trying to pull the blood back towards your feet. To solve this problem, veins have valves in them which can open to allow blood to pass through and close to stop it flowing back down again. Because the blood isn't under as much pressure in the veins, vein walls aren't as thick as artery walls.

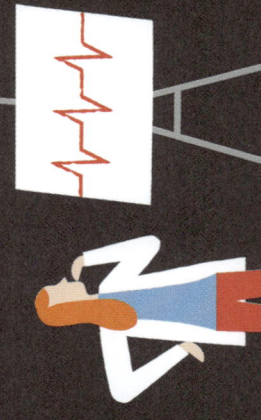

BODY BOOST

Every time your heart beats, the arteries all over your body swell as blood surges into them. You can feel this in places where the arteries are near the surface of the skin. It's called a 'pulse', and the easiest place to feel it is in your wrist. Ask a grown-up to check your pulse and work out the beats per minute when you're completely rested. In children aged one to ten, it's usually between 60 and 110 beats per minute. In older children and adults it's usually between 60 and a 100 beats per minute.

VEINS

ARTERIES

CAPILLARIES

There are three main kinds of blood vessel: arteries, veins and capillaries. **ARTERIES** carry oxygen-rich blood away from the heart to the rest of the body. This is an important job because, without the arteries, the body wouldn't get the oxygen and nutrients from the blood that it needs to work.

The heart powerfully squeezes the blood when it leaves the left ventricle so that it has enough pressure to get around the body, even to far-away places such as your little toe. The walls of arteries are thick, strong and elastic to cope with the pressure. They split in to lots of branches and get smaller and smaller throughout the body, like the little twigs at the end of a branch on a tree. Eventually, they become really tiny capillaries that nourish every cell in the body.

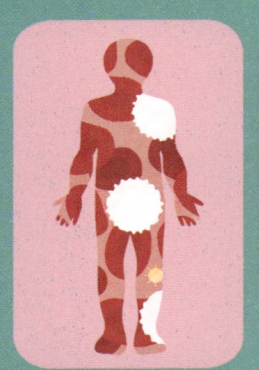

Let's stay inside a vein for the moment and take a look at blood. Close up, we can see that it isn't a thick red liquid but a mixture of different types of cell, all floating in a clear, sticky fluid called plasma. It's incredible stuff!

BRILLIANT BLOOD

Without blood, all the cells in your body would quickly die. As well as carrying oxygen, blood helps the body regulate its temperature, carries nutrients to cells to help them grow, and takes away waste products, such as carbon dioxide.

RED BLOOD CELLS contain haemoglobin, which carries oxygen to the rest of the body's cells. A single red blood cell travels for 400 kilometres in its three-month lifetime. About two million red blood cells are made and another two million old ones are destroyed every single second!

BODY BOOST

If you have anaemia it means that your body doesn't have enough red blood cells. It's a common problem and can be caused by many things, including not eating enough foods containing iron, which is needed to make red blood cells. So help keep your blood healthy by eating foods rich in iron, such as dark green leafy vegetables and meat.

When you cut your finger, sometimes the blood is bright red, and sometimes it's darker. That's because blood carrying oxygen is bright red, and blood without oxygen is dark. Blood looks blue where you can see veins under your skin, but that's just the way the skin absorbs light – your blood is definitely red!

WHITE BLOOD CELL

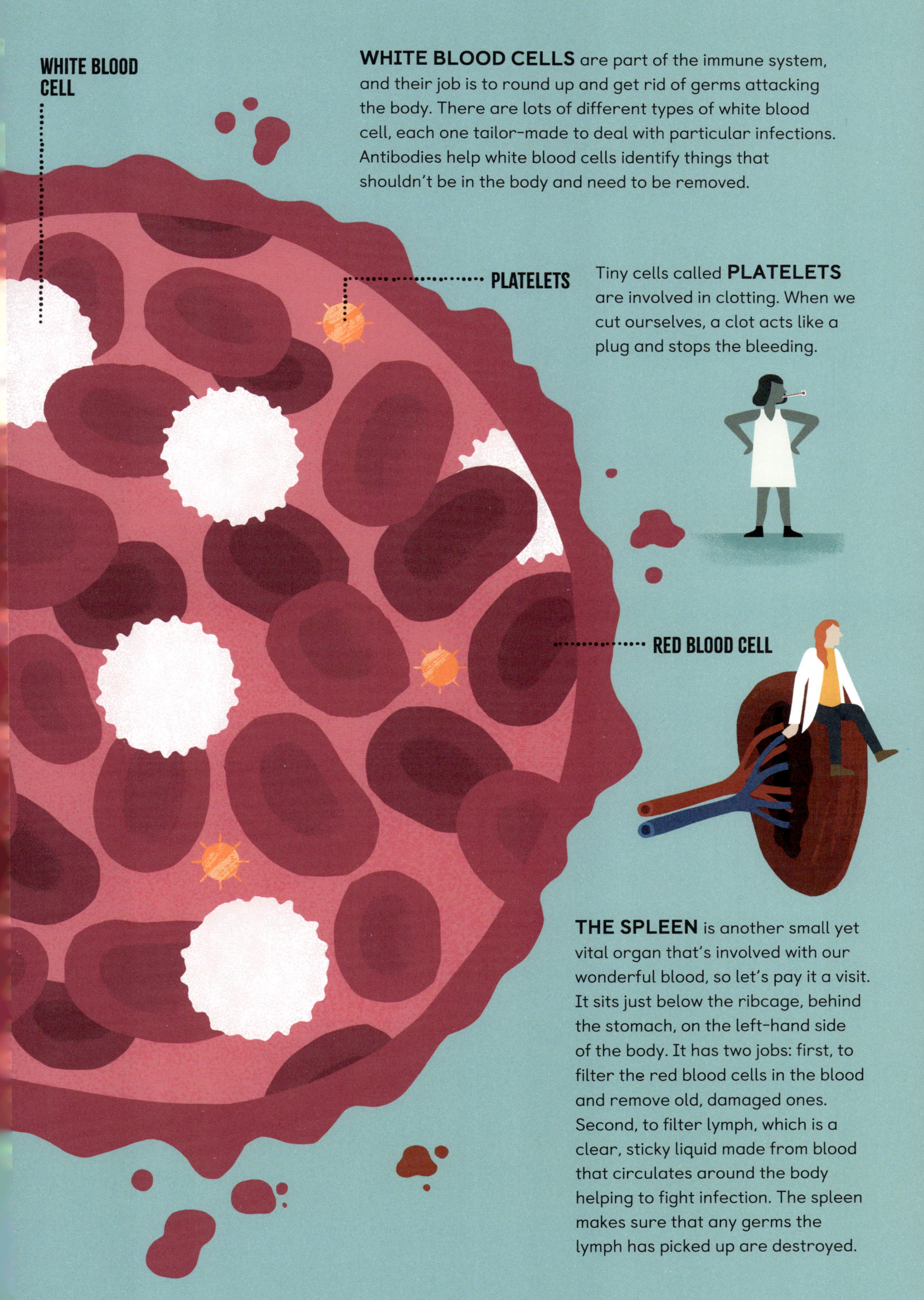

WHITE BLOOD CELLS are part of the immune system, and their job is to round up and get rid of germs attacking the body. There are lots of different types of white blood cell, each one tailor-made to deal with particular infections. Antibodies help white blood cells identify things that shouldn't be in the body and need to be removed.

PLATELETS Tiny cells called **PLATELETS** are involved in clotting. When we cut ourselves, a clot acts like a plug and stops the bleeding.

RED BLOOD CELL

THE SPLEEN is another small yet vital organ that's involved with our wonderful blood, so let's pay it a visit. It sits just below the ribcage, behind the stomach, on the left-hand side of the body. It has two jobs: first, to filter the red blood cells in the blood and remove old, damaged ones. Second, to filter lymph, which is a clear, sticky liquid made from blood that circulates around the body helping to fight infection. The spleen makes sure that any germs the lymph has picked up are destroyed.

SKIN DEEP

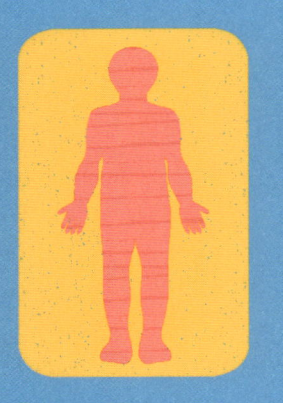

You might not think of it as an organ, but in fact skin is the largest organ in your body. It's pretty amazing – as well as covering and protecting our insides, it helps us keep warm or cool down, it's waterproof and can even repair itself!

Touch is one of your skin's most important jobs. When you stroke a dog, special cells in your skin are stimulated and, using the nerve network, tell your brain that you're touching something warm and furry. Nerve cells in your skin can detect different things, including cold and heat, light pressure, deep pressure, faint touch, pain and stretching.

Skin is made up of lots of different types of cells and tissues, and some of them are only found in the skin. For example, melanocytes make a substance called melanin, which helps protect it from sun damage, and also gives skin its colour. The colour of your skin – dark, light or somewhere in between – depends on the amount of melanin it has.

When skin cells reach the surface of your skin, they die and flake off. So when you look at your hands, you're really looking at dead skin cells! You lose approximately 50,000 flakes of dead skin every minute. Half of all house dust is dead skin cells – yuck!

Between two and four million sweat glands cover your skin, many of them concentrated on the palms of your hands and the soles of your feet. (That's the reason for smelly trainers!) But you sweat for a different reason – to control your body temperature, as it helps you cool down your skin.

And when you're feeling cold, the hairs on your skin might stand up, giving you goosebumps. This happens so air can be trapped next to the skin, which helps to keep us warm.

EPIDERMIS
The outer protective layer of skin.

DERMIS
Contains nerve endings, blood vessels, sweat glands and sebaceous glands. Sebaceous glands produce sebum, your skin's natural moisturiser and waterproofing agent.

BODY BOOST

Exposure to the sun over a long period of time can damage the cells in the skin and sometimes leads to skin cancer. That's why it's so important to use sun cream with a high protection factor, and stay out of the sun or cover up during the hottest part of the day.

SUBCUTANEOUS LAYER
Mostly made up of fat and anchors the skin to the tissue underneath. Hair follicles can grow from this layer.

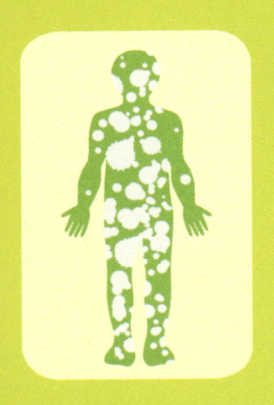

You might not realise it, but at this very moment you are under attack. Germs are desperately trying to get inside your body and set up home, making you sick in the process. Luckily, your body is ready to fight these invaders, using your incredible immune system.

THE DEFENDERS

Your body uses physical barriers to protect itself. Skin is tough and waterproof, so it's hard for bugs to get through it and in to your bloodstream. Tears wash germs out of your eyes. Saliva contains chemicals to kill things that might make you sick if you swallow them. Even the snot up your nose is designed to stop germs from getting in to your airways!

·········· CUT   BLOOD CLOT ··········

Sometimes these defences don't work and a germ manages to sneak in. There's a plan for that too. If you cut yourself, for example, your body's natural repair kit swings in to action. The blood around the wound clots to become thick and sticky, forming a plug to stop more germs from entering. Then white blood cells travel to the wound to kill germs that might already have managed to invade. That's why a cut might feel hot and swollen – it's the blood carrying all the white blood cells to the wound to protect you.

BODY BOOST

We have natural defences against infection and illness, but doctors sometimes give us vaccine injections to protect us from particular diseases. Vaccines work by teaching the body how to recognise a certain germ so that it can respond very quickly if it's ever infected by it. A vaccine puts a weakened or dead version of the germ in to your body, so your body can learn how to destroy the germ. Vaccines have saved millions of lives since they were first discovered.

Lots of white blood cells live in your lymph nodes, which are often found in your armpit or neck. These filter your blood and catch germs. When you're unwell, the nodes sometimes swell up and become painful because of the extra work they're doing to fight the infection. They go down again once the infection is beaten.

The immune system protects your body from all kinds of diseases.

PUS

SCAB

But sometimes the infection is too strong and the white blood cells are overwhelmed. When you get a bad infection, you'll see white and greenish-yellow pus in the cut. The pus is made up of dead white blood cells that have died in the battle against the germs. Yuck! Most of the time though, a blood clot forms and becomes a scab. This protects the wound while the skin repairs itself underneath. When the skin has reformed, the scab becomes itchy and falls off.

FUR AND CLAWS

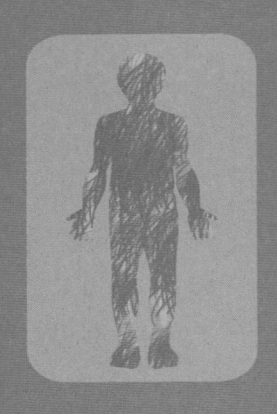

Strange and alarming though it may sound, dead things are growing on you all the time! Even though our hair and nails grow, they're not alive. That's why it doesn't hurt when we cut them.

Let's continue our microscopic adventure in the subcutaneous layer of the skin, where hair starts to grow! You'll see that each hair grows out of a pocket called a hair follicle. At the bottom of the follicle is a root made of a tough, waterproof substance called keratin. As the follicle makes more keratin, the hair grows. Along the follicle are also special glands that produce sebum – an oil that gives our hair shine and can sometimes make it feel greasy.

Hair is thickest on our heads – most people have around 100,000 individual hairs, in fact! But did you know that hair is almost everywhere on our bodies? Some of the hairs are so tiny that you might need a magnifying glass to see them. The only places on your body that aren't covered in hair are your lips, the palms of your hands and the soles of your feet.

BODY BOOST

We use shampoo to remove some of the grease on our hair, and conditioner to help smooth down tiny scales on the hair called cuticles. Sometimes, you can get dandruff, which happens when the skin cells on the scalp produces too many new skin cells and sheds the old ones, which can be seen on your clothes as white flakes. Usually, you can get rid of dandruff with anti-dandruff shampoo.

Nails are the human equivalent of claws. They protect the ends of our fingers, and we use them to scratch or pick at things. Your nails are made of exactly the same thing as your hair – keratin– but it's more tightly packed than in hair, so your nails are harder. The part of the nail we can see is dead, but there is a living part in the fingers and toes called the nail bed, which sits behind and at the bottom of the nail. It's this part that grows. Fingernails grow about 3.5 millimetres each week, while toenails grow even more slowly.

Your nails grow fastest on the hand you use the most!

WONDERFUL GIRLS AND WOMEN

We all look different, but on the inside we're pretty much the same, with the same organs – a stomach, liver, heart and lungs. But girls and women have some organs that boys and men don't have, and vice versa. These are the organs that are involved in reproduction – making babies – and it's a really important part of what our bodies do, because if we didn't make babies, the human race would have died out a long time ago!

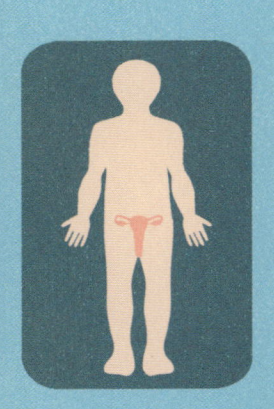

FALLOPIAN TUBES
Run from the ovaries to the uterus. When an egg is released from an ovary, it travels down this tube.

OVARIES
Egg cells are needed to make a baby and they're made in two organs called ovaries. An ovary releases an egg once a month.

BODY BOOST

Periods usually happen once every 28 days or so, and, on average, girls and women bleed around eight teaspoons of blood, which takes a few days to come out. You can use sanitary pads or tampons to soak up the blood but, other than that, you don't need to do anything special, and can do all the activities you'd do at any other time!

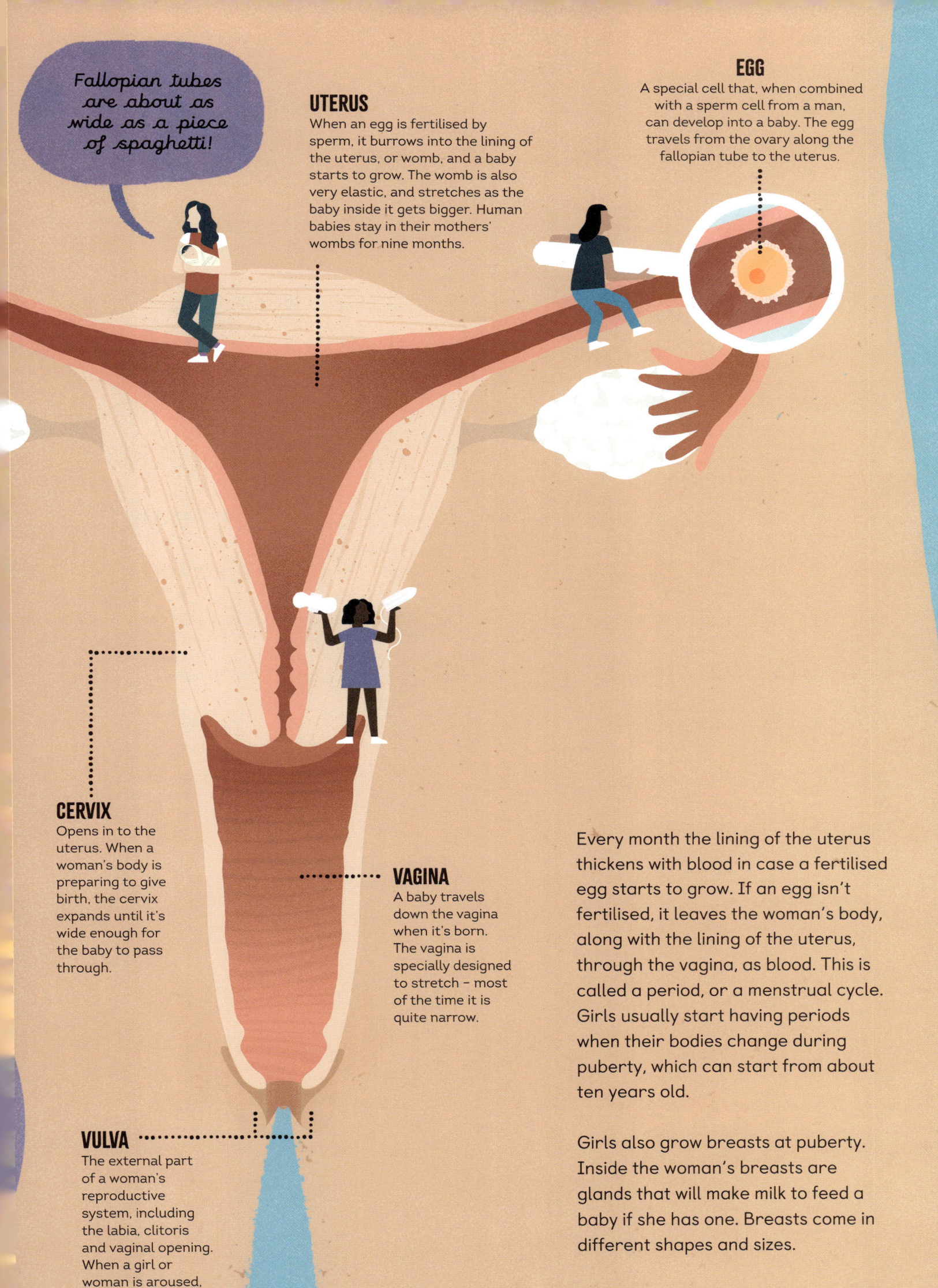

Fallopian tubes are about as wide as a piece of spaghetti!

UTERUS
When an egg is fertilised by sperm, it burrows into the lining of the uterus, or womb, and a baby starts to grow. The womb is also very elastic, and stretches as the baby inside it gets bigger. Human babies stay in their mothers' wombs for nine months.

EGG
A special cell that, when combined with a sperm cell from a man, can develop into a baby. The egg travels from the ovary along the fallopian tube to the uterus.

CERVIX
Opens in to the uterus. When a woman's body is preparing to give birth, the cervix expands until it's wide enough for the baby to pass through.

VAGINA
A baby travels down the vagina when it's born. The vagina is specially designed to stretch – most of the time it is quite narrow.

VULVA
The external part of a woman's reproductive system, including the labia, clitoris and vaginal opening. When a girl or woman is aroused, this area becomes very sensitive.

Every month the lining of the uterus thickens with blood in case a fertilised egg starts to grow. If an egg isn't fertilised, it leaves the woman's body, along with the lining of the uterus, through the vagina, as blood. This is called a period, or a menstrual cycle. Girls usually start having periods when their bodies change during puberty, which can start from about ten years old.

Girls also grow breasts at puberty. Inside the woman's breasts are glands that will make milk to feed a baby if she has one. Breasts come in different shapes and sizes.

MARVELLOUS BOYS AND MEN

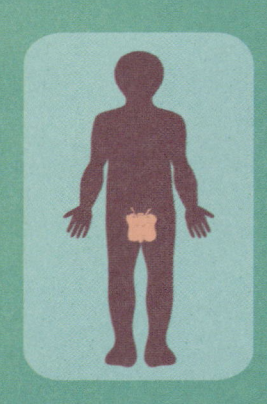

Female reproductive organs are tucked away inside the body. But the body parts unique to men and boys – a penis and testicles – are outside the body.

Boys are born with a foreskin, which is a piece of skin that covers the end of the penis. It's sometimes removed in an operation called a circumcision, which can happen for religious reasons – for example, lots of Jewish and Muslim people are circumcised when they are young. But it can also be removed for medical reasons, if the skin becomes too tight and painful.

When a boy or a man is aroused, the penis stands up and becomes hard. This is called an erection, and is caused by more blood entering the penis, making it swell. Erections often occur on waking, but they can happen any time – on the bus or even during class.

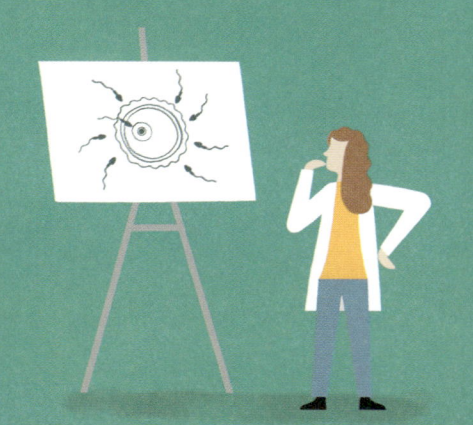

BODY BOOST

When a boy starts puberty, his body begins to make semen, and he might have something called a 'wet dream' – he has an erection and semen comes out of his penis while he's asleep. It doesn't happen to all boys, but it's absolutely normal if it does happen.

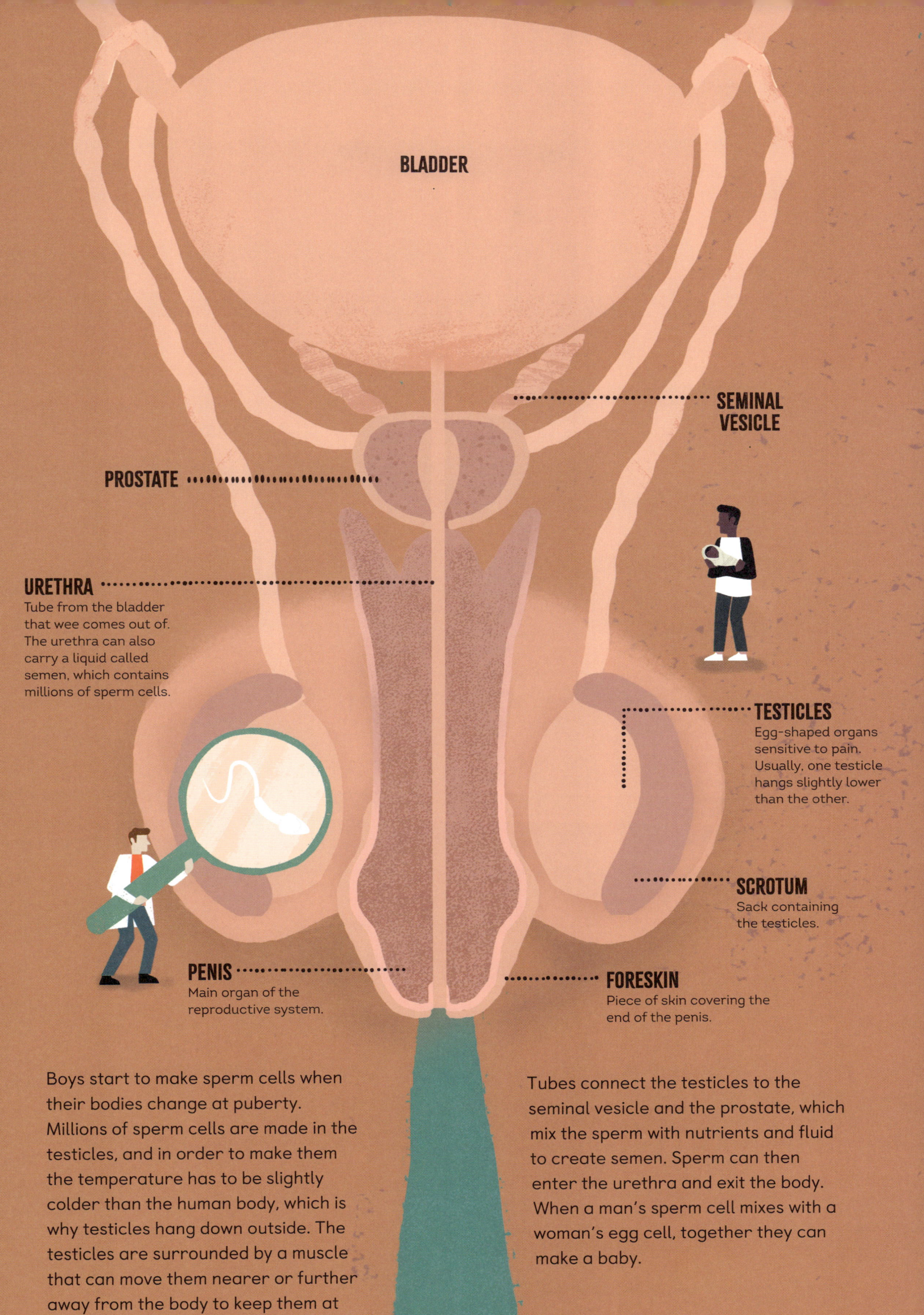

BLADDER

SEMINAL VESICLE

PROSTATE

URETHRA
Tube from the bladder that wee comes out of. The urethra can also carry a liquid called semen, which contains millions of sperm cells.

TESTICLES
Egg-shaped organs sensitive to pain. Usually, one testicle hangs slightly lower than the other.

SCROTUM
Sack containing the testicles.

PENIS
Main organ of the reproductive system.

FORESKIN
Piece of skin covering the end of the penis.

Boys start to make sperm cells when their bodies change at puberty. Millions of sperm cells are made in the testicles, and in order to make them the temperature has to be slightly colder than the human body, which is why testicles hang down outside. The testicles are surrounded by a muscle that can move them nearer or further away from the body to keep them at just the right temperature.

Tubes connect the testicles to the seminal vesicle and the prostate, which mix the sperm with nutrients and fluid to create semen. Sperm can then enter the urethra and exit the body. When a man's sperm cell mixes with a woman's egg cell, together they can make a baby.

NEW LIFE

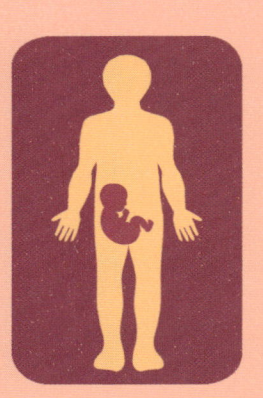

We've nearly reached the end of our journey and we're about to find out about one of the most marvellous things of all about the human body, creating new life.

To make a baby, a woman's egg cell is fertilised by a man's sperm cell. The woman becomes pregnant and the baby, known as a foetus when it's inside the womb, starts to grow.

It's incredible to think that life begins from one tiny fertilised egg cell that is only the size of a full stop! That cell divides up in to two cells. These cells divide again, and again, millions of times. Each time the cells divide, some of them become specialist cells that go on to make the organs we've visited in this book. After around six weeks, the heart begins to beat. At five months, the foetus starts to kick inside the womb. And after nine months, it's a fully formed baby, ready to be born!

The growing foetus lives inside a sac of liquid called amniotic fluid. It can't feed or breathe by itself. Instead, the oxygen and nutrients it needs to grow are passed through a thick tube called the umbilical cord, which is attached to the inside of the womb by a network of blood vessels called the placenta. Your belly button is where your umbilical cord used to be!

MARVELLOUS YOU

So, we've been on quite an adventure. We've peered into the pancreas, looked inside a lung, and even stretched out a strand of DNA. Now that you've explored the human body, I hope you can see just how marvellous it is, just like I did when I first trained to be a doctor. From now on, maybe you'll take the time to appreciate the different body parts that make everything we do possible, from stroking a pet to skateboarding. Perhaps you'll become a doctor one day. Whatever happens, take care of yourself – after all, you are absolutely marvellous!

GLOSSARY

ACID A special type of chemical that reacts with other substances and can dissolve them. The stomach produces acid, which helps to breakdown food and kill germs. Some acids, like vinegar, are weak and taste sour, while others are strong and can burn if you get them on your skin.

AMNIOTIC FLUID The fluid that surrounds a baby as it develops and grows in the woman's womb. The amniotic fluid helps to protect the baby and cushions it from any knocks and bumps.

BACTERIA When you're not feeling well, it might be because of bacteria. These are tiny creatures that are so small they can't be seen without using a microscope, but there are billions of them all over your body. Most of them don't cause any harm, but sometimes bad bacteria can cause infection and make us sick.

BLOODSTREAM The flow of blood inside the blood vessels that whooshes around your body.

CALCIUM A substance that is very important for keeping your bones and teeth strong. It's found in dairy foods like milk and yoghurt, as well as other foods like beans, seeds and green leafy vegetables.

CARBON DIOXIDE A gas that we breathe out into the atmosphere. It's sometimes shortened to the chemical symbol CO_2.

CELL These are the building blocks of your body. They are tiny, and your body is made up of trillions of them. There are lots of different types of cells and each type has a special job to do in the body.

CIRCULATORY SYSTEM This is everything that's involved in moving blood around the body. It includes the heart, which pumps the blood; the arteries, which carry that blood around the body; the capillaries, which surround the cells and then the veins, which carry the blood back to the heart.

DIGESTION breaking down the food we eat into tiny bits that can then be absorbed by the body.

DNA This stands for deoxyribonucleic (say: dee-ox-see-ri-bo-nyoo-clay-ik) acid. It is long strands that look like a twisted ladder, tightly curled up in the nucleus of the cell, that tells the cell what to do. It's like an instruction manual for how to make a person! Everyone's DNA is slightly different, which is what makes us different.

ENZYME This is a special substance that can speed up a chemical reaction. There are different enzymes that do different jobs. For example, some enzymes help the body to break down food in the stomach.

FERTILISATION When an egg cell and a sperm cell join together. The egg is said to be 'fertilised' and from this a baby starts to grow.

FOETUS The medical name for the baby developing in the womb nine weeks after an egg is fertilised until birth. When it is less than eight weeks old it is called an embryo.

GENES Bits of DNA that give information for specific characteristics, like the colour of your hair or how tall you'll be.

GERMS These are tiny little creatures, far too small to see with the naked eye. They can cause disease and illness, making us sick. There are different types of germs, for example bacteria or viruses.

GLANDS These are areas of the body that release hormones or enzymes.

HAEMOGLOBIN This is a chemical in red blood

cells and is what makes them red. It's a very clever substance that helps blood to carry oxygen to all the parts of your body.

IMMUNE SYSTEM This fights infection and keeps our bodies safe from germs that try to attack it.

INSULIN A hormone that is made in the pancreas. It helps to control the amount of sugar in our blood.

MENSTRUAL CYCLE Each month the woman's ovaries release an egg and prepare the womb to look after a developing baby. If the egg is not fertilised, then the egg and the lining of the womb come away and leave the body through the vagina. The next month, the same thing happens. Another name for menstruation is 'period'.

MICROSCOPIC Something so small that it can only be seen by using a microscope – a power machine that makes tiny things look bigger!

NEPHRONS A filtering unit inside the kidney. There are millions of these in the kidney and it's what makes them so good at cleaning and filtering the blood.

NEURONS Special nerve cells. They carry electrical impulses and are the basic unit of the nervous system. There are lots of them in the brain.

NUCLEUS The control centre of every cell. It contains DNA that tells the cell what to do.

ORGAN A part of your body that's made up of different types of tissue that work together. Some organs have just one function – like your eye, which helps you see. Other organs, like your liver, have over 500 different jobs!

OXYGEN This is a gas that's in the air we breathe and cells need it in order to live.

PAPILLAE These are the little fleshy bumps on something. There are lots of papillae on your tongue. They help to grip food and also contain your taste buds, which help us enjoy our food. Yum!

PROTEIN This is needed to build cells and tissues in the body. Your muscles and organs are mostly made of protein. We get protein from what we eat – you can find it in nuts, eggs, meat and fish.

PUBERTY The stage of development when our bodies grow and change, and we mature into an adult body.

REFLEXES These are quick actions that happen without us having to think about them. For example, blinking if an insect flies near your eye.

REPRODUCTIVE SYSTEM These are the parts of the body that are involved in reproduction – in making a baby. The reproductive system is different for a man and a woman.

SUBCUTANEOUS 'Sub' means 'under' and 'cutaneous' means 'skin', so this means anything that is under the skin.

TISSUE A collection of different types of cells that work together.

VITAMIN D This is another chemical that, like calcium, is important for strong teeth and bones. It is also important for the immune system. It is found in food such as dairy products like cheese and also eggs and some vegetables. Our skin can make its own vitamin D when it is exposed to the sun, but be careful not to get sunburned.

INDEX

acid 31, 43, 60
air 42
alcohol 35
alveoli 43
amniotic fluid 58, 60
anaemia 46
antibodies 47
anus 32
aorta 40, 41
asthma 43
arteries 36, 40, 41, 44, 45
atria (singular: atrium) 41
auditory cortex 14

babies 54, 55, 57, 58
backs 18
bacteria 32, 60
balance 23
belly buttons 58
bile 33, 34
birth 54
bladders 11, 36, 38–39, 57
bleeding 47
blood 6, 11, 13, 31, 32, 35, 36, 37, 40, 41, 42, 43, 44–45, 46–47, 51, 54, 55, 56
blood vessels 11, 25, 26, 43, 44–45, 49, 58
bloodstream 4, 31, 32, 37, 40, 42, 44, 60
bone marrow 13
bones 6, 10, 12–13, 18, 23
bottoms 32
boys 56–57 see also men
brains 13, 14–15, 16, 17, 18, 19, 21, 23, 25, 28, 31
brainstem 14
breasts 55
breathing 10, 14, 25, 41, 42
Broca's area 14
bronchi (singular: bronchus) 42, 43
bronchioles 42, 43

calcium 12, 60
canines 27
capillaries 44, 45
carbon dioxide 6, 42, 43, 46, 60
cardiac muscle 11, 40
cartilage 13, 18, 19
cell membranes 6
cells 6–7, 8, 13, 15, 17, 21, 23, 25, 30, 31, 37, 38, 40, 42, 43, 44, 46, 47, 48, 58, 60

central nervous system 14
cervix 54
chests 42
circulatory system 40, 60
circumcision 56
clitoris 54
clotting 47, 50
coccyx 19
cochleas 23
colds 25
colour 21, 48
communication 11, 15
cones (eye cells) 21
constipation 33
contact lenses 21
corneas 21
cuticles 52
cuts 50
cytoplasm 6

dandruff 52
dentine 26, 27
dentists 27
dermis 47
detrusor muscle 38
diabetes 30, 31
diaphragm 42
diarrhoea 33
digestion 26, 30–31, 32–33, 60
digestive system 7
disease 51
DNA (deoxyribonucleic acid) 8, 60
doctors 4, 12, 20, 35, 39, 51, 59
drinking 37

ear canals 23
eardrums 23
ears 14, 17, 22–23
egg cells (eggs) 54, 55, 57, 58
emotion 15
enamel 26, 27
energy 6, 26, 34, 42
enzymes 28, 31, 32, 60
epiglottis 29
erections 56
exercise 12, 41, 43
eyes 7, 9, 11, 14, 17, 20–21

Fallopian tubes 54, 55
fats 33, 34, 49
female reproductive system 54–55
fertilisation 55, 58, 60
filtering 36, 37, 47, 51

fingers 53
focusing 11, 21
foetuses 58, 60
follicles 49, 51
foreskin 56, 57
food 7, 12, 25, 26, 28, 29, 30, 31, 32, 33, 41, 46

gall bladder 33, 34
genes 8–9, 60
germs 25, 27, 33, 43, 47, 50, 51, 60
girls 54–55 see also women
glands 20, 35, 49, 52, 55, 60
glasses 21
goosebumps 49
gullet see oesophagus
gums 27
guts see intestines

haemoglobin 46, 60
hair 9, 23, 49, 52–53
hearing 17, 22–23
heartbeats 40
hearts 10, 11, 13, 36, 40–41, 43, 44, 45, 58
hippocampus 14
hormones 14
hypothalamus 14

illness 51
images 21
immune system 47, 50–51, 61
incisors 27
infection 25, 33, 47, 51
information 16, 17, 18, 19, 21, 23, 28, 38
inhalers 43
injections 31, 51
inner ear 23
insulin 30, 31, 34, 61
intestines 7, 11, 28, 30, 31, 32–33, 34
iris 20
iron 46
jaws 26
joints 13

keratin 52, 53
kidney dialysis 37
kidneys 36–37, 38, 39

language 14
large intestines 32, 33 see also intestines

62

legs 10, 41
lenses 21
ligaments 18
light 21
livers 7, 33, 34-35
lungs 10, 13, 41, 42-43
lymph 47, 51

male reproductive system 56-57
medication and medicine 30, 43
medulla 14
melanin 48
melanocytes 48
memories 14, 15, 25
men 56-57, 58 see also boys
menstrual cycle 55, 61
microscopic 61
middle ear 23
milk 55
milk teeth 27
molars 27
mouths 27, 28-29, 30, 42
movement 10
mucus 25, 31, 43
muscles 10-11, 13, 14, 16, 17, 18, 19, 20, 31, 38, 41, 42
musculoskeletal system 10

nails 52
necks 18
nephrons 37, 61
nerves 16-17, 18, 19, 21, 25, 26, 28, 38, 48, 49
neurons (nerve cells) 6, 15, 16, 48, 61
noses 17, 24-25, 42
nostrils 24
nuclei (singular: nucleus) 6, 8, 61
nutrients 6, 34, 37, 44, 45, 47, 58

oesophagus (gullet) 7, 28, 29
optic nerve 21
organs 6, 7, 13, 17, 31, 33, 34, 40, 47, 48, 49, 54, 56, 57, 61
ossicles 23
osteoblasts and osteoclasts 13
otoscopes 23
outer ear 23
ovaries 54
oxygen 6, 40, 41, 42, 43, 44, 45, 46, 58, 61

pain 48
pancreas 30, 31, 32, 34
papillae 28, 29, 61
pelvic-floor muscles 38
penises 56, 57
periods 54, 55

pituitary gland 14
placenta 58
plaster casts 13
plasma 46
platelets 47
poo 32, 33
pregnancy 58
premolars 27
pressure 48
protein 7, 61
puberty 55, 56, 57, 61
pulmonary artery 41
pulp 26
pulse 45
pupils 20, 21
pus 51

red blood cells 6, 35, 46
reflexes 17, 19, 61
reproduction 54-55
reproductive systems 54-55, 56-57, 61
retinas 21
ribcages 13
rods (eye cells) 21

saliva (spit) 26, 28, 29, 30, 50
salt 41
scabs 51
scalp 52
sclera 20
scrotums 57
sebaceous glands 49, 52
sebum 49, 52
semen 56, 57
semicircular canals 23
senses 16, 17, 20, 21, 22, 23, 24, 25, 28
sensors 28
sensory cortex 14
sight 17, 20-21
skeletal muscles 10
skeleton 13
skin 17, 48-49, 50, 52
skin cancer 49
skin cells 52
skull 13
sleep 15
small intestines 32, 33 see also intestines
smell 17, 24-25
smooth muscle 11, 28
snot 25, 50
sound waves 23
sperm 55, 57, 58
sperm duct 57
spinal cords 14, 18, 19
spine 18-19

spleen 47
stomach acid 31, 43
stomachs 7, 11, 28, 29, 30, 31, 32
subcutaneous layer 49, 52, 61
sugar 27, 30, 31, 34
sun 48, 49
swallowing 28, 29
sweat glands 49
sweating 37, 49
systems 7, 10, 54-55, 56-57

taste 17, 25, 28
taste buds 28, 29
tears 20, 50
teeth 26-27, 28, 30
temperature 46, 48, 49, 57
tendons 10
testicles 56, 57
throat 28, 43
tissue 6, 7, 13, 18, 27, 48, 61
toes 53
toilets 33, 39
tongues 17, 28
toothache 27
touch 14, 17, 48, 54
toxins 35
trachea (windpipe) 29, 42, 43
twins 9

umbilical cord 58
ureter 36, 37, 38, 39
urethra 38, 39, 57
urine (wee) 36, 37, 38, 39, 57
uterus (womb) 54, 55, 58

vaccines 51
vaginas 55
valves 40, 44
veins 36, 40, 44, 45, 46
vena cava 40
ventricles 41, 45
vertebrae 18, 19
visual cortex 14
vitamin D 12, 61
vulvas 55

waste 6, 36, 37, 44, 46
water 32, 37
wax (earwax) 23
wee see urine
'wet dreams' 56
white blood cells 47, 50, 51
windpipe see trachea
wisdom teeth 27
womb see uterus
women 54-55, 58 see also girls

X-rays 12

63

For Henry and Monty.
– M.P

For my Mum – without whom, this book
would not have been finished.
– C.M

First published in Great Britain in 2019 by
Wren & Rook

Text copright © Max Pemberton, 2019
Illustration copyright © Chris Madden, 2019
All rights reserved.

ISBN: 978 1 5263 6119 6
E-book ISBN: 978 1 5263 6120 2
10 9 8 7 6 5 4 3 2 1

MIX
Paper from
responsible sources
FSC® C104740

Wren & Rook
An imprint of Hachette Children's Group
Part of Hodder & Stoughton
Carmelite House
50 Victoria Embankment
London EC4Y 0DZ
An Hachette UK Company
www.hachette.co.uk
www.hachettechildrens.co.uk

Publishing Director: Debbie Foy
Senior Editors: Liza Miller and Laura Horsley
Art Director: Laura Hambleton
Designer: Peter Clayman
Printed in China

Every effort has been made to clear copyright. Should there be any inadvertent
omission, please apply to the publisher for rectification.

The website addresses (URLs) included in this book were valid at the time of
going to press. However, it is possible that contents or addresses may have
changed since the publication of this book. No responsibility for any such
changes can be accepted by either the author or the publisher.

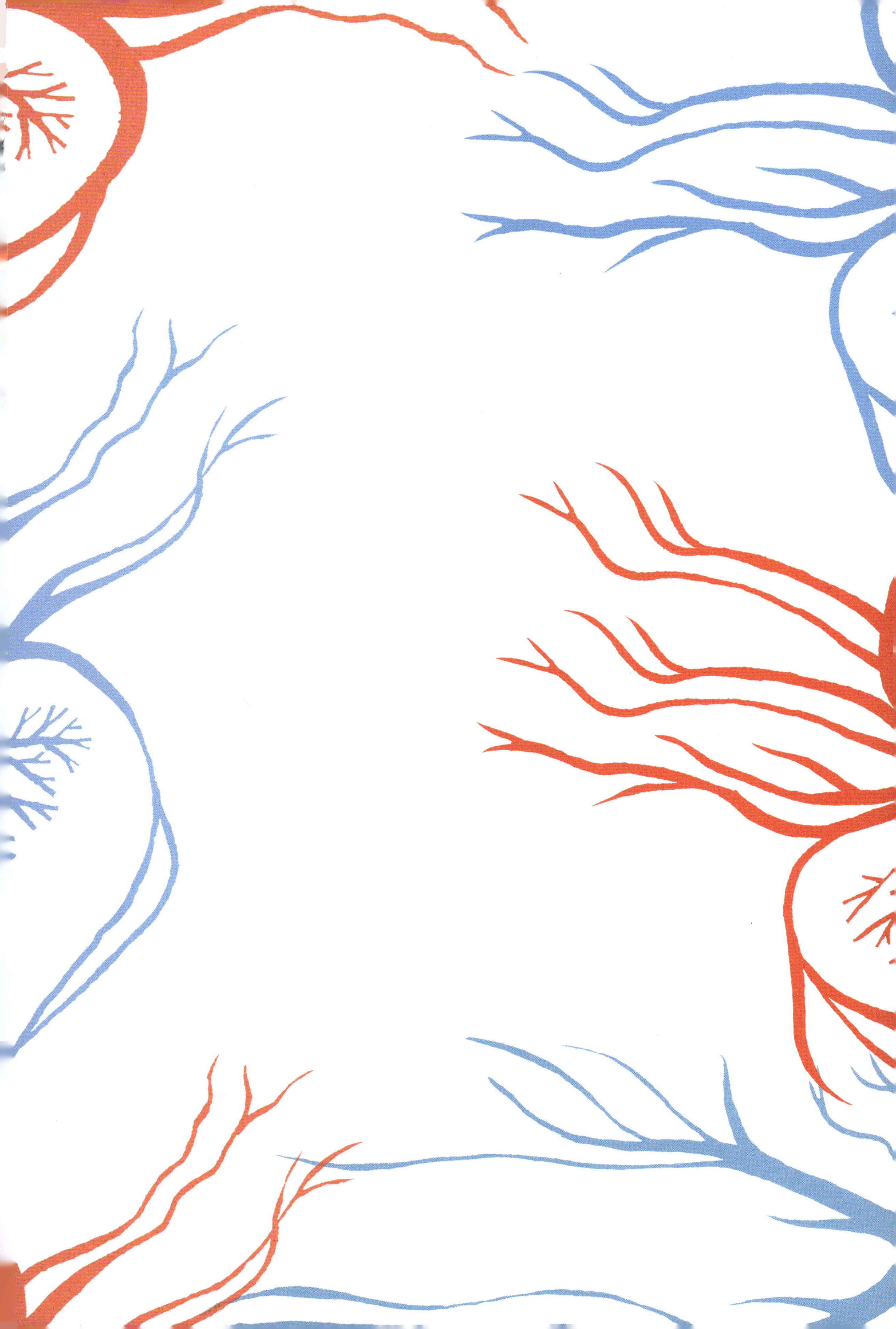